SPIRITUAL WARFARE AND YOUR CHILDREN

RAY BEESON & KATHI MILLS

Thomas Nelson Publishers
Nashville

Published in Nashville, Tennessee, by Thomas Nelson, Inc., Publishers, and distributed in Canada by Word Communications, Ltd., Richmond, British Columbia, and in the United Kingdom by Word (UK), Ltd., Milton Keynes, England.

We have tried to present stories as accurately as possible, although many details, including names and genders, have been changed in order to protect identities.

Library of Congress Cataloging-in-Publication Data

Beeson, Ray.
    Spiritual warfare and your children / Ray Beeson and Kathi Mills.
        p.   cm.
    Includes bibliographical references.
    ISBN 0-8407-3490-5 (pbk.)
    1. Family—Religious life.   2. Parenting—Religious aspects-
-Christianity.   3. Spiritual warfare.   I. Mills, Kathi, 1948–
II. Title.
BV4526.2.B426   1993
248.8'45—dc20   93–8939
                                                                              CIP

Printed in the United States of America

1 2 3 4 5 6 7 — 99 98 97 96 95 94 93

FROM RAY

To Ralyn, a wonderful young lady
whose earlier years of struggle were
not only tough on her parents but on
her as well. Your dad loves you.

FROM KATHI

To Chris, once a child of promise,
        soon a child of the King.
You are deeply loved.

Contents

▼▼▼▼▼

Acknowledgments

We would like to thank the many people who helped bring this book to completion. First, our spouses, Linda and Larry, were so patient and supportive during the long hours necessary to complete a manuscript of this nature. Next, a number of people gave of their time and expertise to critique the manuscript through several stages of rewriting and revision: Lou and Lynda Blaise, Bill and Vicki Ballard, Carol Beckerdite, Dan and Julie Carobine, Hank and Myrene Morris, Patsy Oquist, Kent Kelley, Scott Gossenberger, Gary Rieben, Jim and Hope Deck. And, finally, many families so willingly shared their stories of struggle and triumph to breathe life into these pages.

Thank you all.

Foreword

▼▼▼▼ _____

A famous preacher, a good friend of mine, entered the classy restaurant with his wife and teenaged son. He was shown to a good table, of course. They didn't attract much attention, though a few recognized the minister, and nodded with approval. The waiter came, took their order, and soon their food was before them.

Without warning, the son stood, loudly tapped his spoon against his glass, attracting the attention of everybody in the restaurant. "Everybody be quiet for a minute, will you? My dad doesn't want to just eat lunch—he wants to pray first." There was immense sarcasm in his voice, and not a little anger.

He sat down, looking around the room with a defiant expression, while his mom and dad, their faces flushed with embarrassment, bowed their heads and silently breathed a blessing over their food.

To everyone in the restaurant, the situation was crystal clear. Mom and Dad were accustomed to having a quiet prayer of thanks over their food, even in a restaurant, and their son resented it. He seemed to take fiendish delight in embarrassing them quite publicly.

Is there a parent looking at this page who can't empathize with that poor embarrassed minister and his wife? And even sympathize with the rebellious son? Though this situation was extreme, haven't we all been embarrassed, both parents and children, by the *war* that seems to rage, even in the best of families?

In today's society, psychologists, and "child-rearing experts" prescribe a permissive and "understanding" attitude toward wayward, headstrong, and "independent" children, and even advise that foot-stomping, red-faced rage and rebellion may be a "good thing," developing character and independence in a child.

But the words of God Himself say otherwise and reflect His creator-wise attitude and advice about the wayward tendencies of children. It's not easy for us parents to take today, is it? Many scriptures run totally against the grain of our society. What about this?

> For rebellion is as the sin of witchcraft,
> And stubbornness is as iniquity and idolatry.
>
> (1 Sam. 15:23 NKJV)

I strongly encourage you to read every word of the excellent book that follows this foreword. I think—I know—every concerned parent with kids still at home ought to devour every word.

You see, the above Scripture passage underscores a very important, fundamental and inescapable truth: God Himself is greatly concerned about the family, and does not intend that we accept or encourage or even put up with rebellion in a child. Why? It's a corruptive, corroding, destructive, tragic _force;_ and even worse, it is devised by the consummate Rebel, the accuser of the brethren, Lucifer himself who rebelled openly against God, and caused the downfall of the first family—and consequently all of mankind.

Insidious, deep-seated, and angry rebellion is, at its core, equivalent to witchcraft—which is _inviting_ the enemy of our souls to step in and wreak havoc in our circumstances. Yes, it's extremely commonplace, and we don't like to think that our own precious children might be subject to such an evil force, but the Lord Himself has revealed to us the seriousness of the situation.

Thank God for Jesus! Consider the desperate father of Mark 9, who brought his _obviously demon possessed son_ to Jesus. His behavior was far worse than that of the minister's son in the restaurant, and probably worse than anything you ever saw from your child at home or otherwise.

Jesus asked the father, "How long has this been happening to him?" And he said, "From childhood." And he went on to plead, "If You can do _anything,_ have compassion on us and help us." Can you, parent, identify with that? Jesus said to him, "If you can believe, all things are possible to him who believes."

Immediately the father of the child cried out and said with tears, "Lord, I believe; help my unbelief!"

You can read for yourself that Jesus commanded an evil spirit to come out of the boy, and though he appeared to fall like a dead person at first, the demon did leave the boy, and his father joyfully took him away.

And Jesus concluded the episode by saying—please listen, concerned parent—"This kind can come out by nothing but prayer and fasting."

Shirley and I raised four wonderful girls, right here in Hollywood, California, and in the context of the entertainment community, with all the sordid influences you can imagine. Like the father of the demon-possessed boy, we early cried out to God, and asked Jesus for help! We *knew* we would never make it through the shark infested waters and get our girls safely to shore without *divine* aid. Thank God, He steered us by His Word and His Spirit into powerful and effective spiritual approaches to rebellion and child rearing, not just human, physical, or psychological means. And though we still made plenty of mistakes, yes, the good Lord gave us insights and direction and methods, by His Word and through the inspiration of the Holy Spirit, and helped us bring our four daughters to fine Christian maturity, and to their marriage partners as chaste young women. Praise the Living God!

Friend, God invented the family and is the ultimate parent. He knows what rebellious kids are like and what to do about it. Authors Ray Beeson and Kathi Mills, like Shirley and I, have slugged it out in the trenches, found out a lot about what does and doesn't work, and offer the benefit of their rich experience to you.

Read and be blessed. Call on God to help you—and He will.

Pat Boone
Beverly Hills, California

Introduction

❖ Someone once said that deciding to have a child is like deciding to let your heart walk around outside your body for the rest of your life. There is a lot of truth in that. When God gave us children, He also gave us a love and concern for them that all the definitions in the world cannot adequately describe. The affection known only to a parent is beyond words. When our children laugh, we laugh. When they hurt, we hurt. When they cry, we cry. They become a part of us in ways never imagined.

And yet, even as our children provide such happiness and joy to our lives, they can also be the source of our deepest pain. That very pain was the catalyst that helped draw our two families together and prompted the writing of this book.

RAY'S STORY_____

My wife, Linda, and I have four children, so we are no strangers to the struggles of parenting. A newspaper account of a car accident involving four young people related that pain all too well since two of those four young people were our own daughters. The car in which they were riding went out of control and hit a lightpole. Amanda, nine, was wearing her seatbelt, yet apparently she still hit the headrest or seatback in front of her and sustained facial injuries. Amy, our fifteen year old, was not wearing a seatbelt and hit the dash and windshield. Her injuries were much more severe. Thankfully they were not life-threatening, for which we are tremendously relieved and grateful. This incident, however, served as a vivid reminder of the pain that often accompanies parenting.

When the pain comes about in a somewhat innocent and unwarranted way, as in the case of this accident, we parents would gladly take our child's place if it were possible. Most parents can identify with this feeling. But when pain comes about in other ways, such as rebellion, the pain is just as bad, maybe worse, and much more difficult to identify with. Wayward young people create emotional heartaches that tear at your insides until you think you will die. And this is exactly the way I felt about the pain that came into our lives as a result of my oldest daughter's rebellion.

When Linda and I were first married, we looked forward to having children. Within a year, Ralyn was born. That six-pound eight-ounce, shriveled up, reddish-looking little wonder looked nothing like the beautiful young woman she is today.

As much as I wanted children, I was at first uneasy about holding such a fragile package. Soon, however, I learned that babies are quite stout and won't break all that easily. As each succeeding child came along, I discovered that they really are slightly more hearty than the average china doll. And so, with the care and caution necessary to protect each child from harm, I began to enjoy the wonders of what my wife and I had brought into the world. Each child added to the blessings of parenting.

What fun it was to hold them in the air while lying on my back, playing airplane. Swoosh! I'd bank them to the right and then to the left. Then a slight dive bomb and that indescribable smile that says, "Do it again, Daddy, this is fun!"

Soon came the additional joy of convincing them that the horrible smelling stuff in the baby food jar was really good for them. Airplane time again. Only this time the airplane was a spoonful of goo. I would hold it high and fly it around in the air overhead; as soon as the mouth opened, the plane would make its landing. I cannot tell you how many times that plane came oozing back out of the hangar. I really do admire the baby food people, but I am just thankful they do not cook for me.

But children grow up. And, because my wife and I are Christians and believe that our children should be raised in the fear and admonition of the Lord, we made a public confession of our commitment to their training. Our church calls it a "dedication." Within the first month or so of Ralyn's birth, we stood—two proud parents, baby Ralyn, and our pastor—before the congregation to say to the Lord and to anybody else listening, that we were giving this child to God. We did the same for the rest of our children, as well.

In the meantime, while she was still in our care, we agreed on that dedication day to do our best to raise her correctly so that she might become a responsible adult and learn to love and respect the Lord. After all, the Scripture affirmed that if you train up a child in the way he should go, when he is old he will not depart out of that way (see Prov. 22:6).

I have no intention of making light of Scripture. I only wish to point out that I assumed things in this matter that Scripture does not teach. My daughter would not turn out properly without some hard work on our parts. And she would have the God-given right to make choices that would be contrary to what we wanted, and at times to what God wanted. Our commitment to being good parents was not a guarantee that she would not exercise her right to rebel.

For the first fifteen years of her life, Ralyn appeared to be a normal, although slightly strong-willed, child. Nothing we could not handle, and nothing that caused much alarm. She was bright, got good grades in school, loved the Lord, loved her parents, and for all practical purposes, appeared to be on the road to success.

Late one night, however, I returned home from a meeting to find my wife deeply disturbed. Ralyn was not home and Linda had not seen her all evening.

For some reason our daughter had not shown up earlier that evening where expected. She had made a brief, emotionless phone call to say she would not be home that night. Nor did she return the next night or the next. In fact, we did not see her for five days. When she finally returned home, she was not the same person. She had had an obvious personality change; certain elements of her character had been altered. She exhibited contempt for much of our parental responsibility for direction of her life. She wanted to be free of our guidance as well as all her own personal responsibility. She certainly did not want anyone, especially her parents, telling her what to do. Her defiance led her to drop out of school and eventually disappear again, this time for a much longer period of time.

We were devastated. What happened? Where did we go wrong? What should we do? The questions seemed endless, often playing themselves over and over in our minds until we felt as if we were losing our sanity. Guilt, shame, embarrassment, blame, confusion, hurt, anxiety, pain—that was our steady diet, and not for just one day. It went on for years. Whenever hope seemed to appear on the horizon, a new storm quickly washed it out to sea.

At times like these you hurt, and the pain is multiplied in your spouse and in your other children, as well. Our third child, Amy, and I were watching TV one night. She was about six or seven years old at the time and had crawled up into my lap to be close to me. Soon we were wrapped up in the scenarios of the make-believe television world. Suddenly, Amy burst into tears, crying uncontrollably. When she finally calmed down, she sobbed, "I'll never get to be in Ralyn's wedding." For some reason she concluded that our situation would not soon return to normal. Very obviously the pain of her sister's rejection of us as a family took its toll on even one of the youngest members.

---- ◆

And that pain goes on. In countless homes across our land, families of all races, creeds, and social status are ravaged by the pain of hurting and hurtful children. No one is immune. If you have children, you are fair game for this agonizing experience.

KATHI'S STORY

I too can relate to both kinds of parental pain: that which is inflicted upon our children through no fault of their own and that which results from their open rebellion.

Because I did not become a Christian until I was twenty-six years old, my first marriage began—and ended—while I was yet an unbeliever. By the time I was twenty, I was a single parent with two small sons to raise. Due to a recurring battle with cancer, for some time I could not care for my children and was forced to send them to live with their father. Not only did I suffer as a result of this separation, but so did my children. To this day I hurt when I see the lingering effects of that separation taking its toll on their lives. But that kind of parental pain is experienced apart from anything a child may have done. I soon learned about the other kind of parental pain—the kind that comes as a result of a child's open rebellion.

By the time my third son was born, I was remarried and had become a Christian. Naively, I believed that, because I was now a child of God, my own child would be spared from any serious problems. How wrong I was!

Although Chris was a true source of delight to me throughout his growing up years, something happened when he turned fifteen that made me wonder if someone had stolen my once sweet and loving child and replaced him with a more than slightly obnoxious substitute. Suddenly he wanted nothing to do with us anymore. His new friends would sit outside in their cars and honk their horns for him, rather than come inside. When we insisted that they come to the door before allowing Chris to leave with them, they seldom spoke and would not look us in the eye. Forbidding him to associate with these newfound friends was not the answer either. They simply stopped coming to the house, and Chris would leave and meet them elsewhere. We tried to tell ourselves that this sort of behavior was "normal," that all teens go through a phase of breaking away from their families, that these new friends of his were just a part of his "declaring his independence." But things soon went from bad to worse. From a child who once received awards at school, Chris now behaved in such a way that I received almost weekly phone calls from school officials. Suspensions and failing grades became a way of life.

We tried everything: threatening, punishing, bribing, rewarding, counseling. Nothing seemed to work. The tension in the house was palpable, the strain almost unbearable. Contrary to everything I had ever believed or dreamed, we finally came to the point of sending him away to live elsewhere for a time. It was incredibly difficult for all of us, and yet there seemed to be no other choice.

Chris, of course, resisted this move at first. Recently, however, he has admitted that he can see that it was necessary. And now, slowly, our relationship has begun to improve.

One thing I have learned from all this is that, no matter how old or how far away your children might be, you never stop being a parent. Daily for as long as I have been a Christian, I pray for each of my children. But every now and then, I sense an urgency to stop whatever I am doing and pray specifically for protection for either one or all of them. One Friday afternoon after Chris had moved away, that very urgency overwhelmed me. I sensed immediately that Chris was in some sort of danger. I dropped to my knees and prayed from the depths of my heart for this son whom I love so dearly. I did not stop praying until the feeling of urgency had passed and I felt that Chris would be all right.

The following Monday I discovered why I had felt the need to pray for Chris's protection. It seems he had plans to go out with four of his friends on Saturday evening. At the last minute, he decided to stay home instead. That night there was an accident, and three of those four young people were killed.

Coincidence? We do not think so. We believe that all Christians have the ability to hear and respond to that still small voice of the Holy Spirit within as He warns us and calls us to prayer.

♦

A War Is Going On

Prayer is the mightiest weapon parents can employ in the protection and guidance of their children. We dare not ignore nor neglect it, particularly in view of some pretty disturbing things happening in our land:

- Next to traffic accidents, gunfire is the most common cause of death for U.S. residents aged 15 to 19; it is the most frequent cause of death for blacks in that age range.[1]
- In 1990, there were 1,355,638 males and 398,904 females under the age of 18 arrested in the United States.[2]
- Sexually transmitted diseases (STDs) infect 3 million teenagers annually.[3]

- Of every 1,000 births in 1988, 9.9 percent were to unmarried females under the age of fifteen.[4]
- Within the 14 states reporting to the National Center for Health Statistics, the abortion rate in 1988 was 325.4 abortions per 1,000 live births; one-fourth of those [induced] abortions were to women under the age of twenty.[5]
- Twenty-nine percent of fifteen-year-old girls, 81 percent of nineteen-year-old girls, 72 percent of seventeen-year-old boys, and 88 percent of nineteen-year-old boys are sexually active.[6]

Shocking statistics. Yet we hear about these children constantly, this current generation of young people whom we believe are under siege by a ruthless enemy. They are being kidnapped, abused, maimed, and murdered at unprecedented rates; but they are also running away, being arrested, committing suicide, and becoming involved in substance abuse, gangs, and satanic cults. However, as tragic as these statistics are, until the pain becomes our own, we don't really relate—nor do we begin to understand how crucial it is to recognize the possibility of demonic activity within our children's lives.

For you see, a war is going on. And, whether we like it or not, our kids are one of the main targets. While most of us are trying to figure out how to make a living or just get on in life, big-gun strategies are being formed in another realm with our children in their sights.

While parts of the church continue to question the reality of the work of demons, much of the rest of the world is out for a full-scale examination. Interest in the supernatural and an ever-increasing popularity with satanism, the new age movement, and the occult are at an all-time high. This is not a rediscovery of a static arena that comes and goes as people look for answers to life; it is a response to the advancement of an age-old war—one about to end, according to the Scriptures.

The war is all around us and it is heating up. It is a war in which "our struggle is not against flesh and blood, but against the rulers, against the authorities, against the powers of this dark world and against the spiritual forces of evil in the heavenly realms" (Eph. 6:12).

Demons are not figments of human imagination. Nor are they concepts or ideas or a description of the corporate evil found in mankind. They are real entities with one goal in mind—to destroy you and your children. Their lies and accusations create deep-seated emotional problems in the lives of countless young people, and only an encounter with Truth will set them free.

The apostle Peter acknowledged that "Your enemy the devil prowls around like a roaring lion looking for someone to devour" (1 Peter 5:8). Much of the negative behavior we see in society today is nothing less than the work of demons.

Notice what the Scripture says about some of that negative behavior:

But mark this: There will be terrible times in the last days. People will be lovers of themselves, lovers of money, boastful, proud, abusive, *disobedient to their parents,* ungrateful, unholy, without love, unforgiving, slanderous, without self-control, brutal, not lovers of the good, treacherous, rash, conceited, lovers of pleasure rather than lovers of God—having a form of godliness but denying its power. Have nothing to do with them.

(2 Tim. 3:1–5, italics added)

Then notice also what the Scripture says about the influence of Satan and his demons on humanity:

We know that we are children of God, and that the whole world is under the control of the evil one.

(1 John 5:19)

It is the Gospel that frees a person from bondage to the enemy. At the same time the Gospel opens up to us an incredible war in which we fight as soldiers under Jesus Christ. The apostle Paul said, "I have fought the good fight" (2 Tim. 4:7); Jesus is referred to as the "captain of our salvation" (Heb. 2:10 NKJV); we are told to "put on the full armor of God" (Eph. 6:11).

Strategy for Battle

Fighting a war effectively is not possible until we understand what we are up against. In the pages that follow we hope you will realize a strategy to help in overcoming the hideous design of the enemy of our soul against our children—maybe one of your own.

At the same time, we hope you will not be frightened by this approach. Although demonic activity is real and seems to be increasing in intensity, this book is not meant to frighten you, but rather to alert you to the problem, and then to help you find solutions in the areas you are affected. Most of all, the book was written to encourage you, to give you hope in the midst of trouble. Jesus is our hope, and our prayer is that He will shine so brightly as you read that your darkness will be dispelled by His love. He knows and heals all our pain, including the pain of parents who are often deeply affected by the lives of their own beloved children.

One more thing before we begin. The goals of our book—to encourage hurting parents and to point to the possibility of demonic activity in the lives of many troubled teenagers—were not easy goals to meet. Within both secular and Christian communities, points of view for dealing with troubled lives differ drastically. We have been concerned that differences among Christians have escalated into deep divisions within the body of Christ.

One issue concerns the psychology and self-help/ recovery movement that has become so popular over the last decade. Christians see the issues from two polarized viewpoints. On one side stand those who fear that secular psychology is replacing biblical teaching.

They see little need for counselors or therapists, asserting that we only come to truly understand ourselves as we see ourselves in God's eyes as expressed in the Bible. In other words we don't need anything but good preaching and teaching from the Scriptures. On the other side are those who believe that people must reach a deeper understanding of themselves if ever they are to begin to overcome their many problems. They believe that psychology is the tool that will help them achieve that deeper understanding.

Although we do not discount the good that can come from biblically based counseling and recovery groups—as we are both involved in those professions to a degree—we believe that, ultimately, all of life's answers are found solely within the authority of the Scriptures. In and of itself, the self-help/recovery movement simply cannot produce the results necessary for a balanced, healthy life.

We are not alone in our thinking. A recent article in the Los Angeles Times pointed out that several long-time proponents of the self-help/recovery movement have begun to question its effectiveness. At the same time, Jane Middelton-Moz, a lecturer and best-selling author on the subject, warns against throwing "the baby out with the bath water."

"Thousands of people have been helped by the movement," she emphasizes, yet cautions that she believes codependency "has proliferated too far. . . . If you remain in a dynamic of defining yourself as damaged, you haven't recovered."[7]

Still, many experts in the field praise the movement for lifting the veil of secrecy, bringing public awareness to certain long-avoided topics—incest, alcoholism, drug addiction, spousal abuse, etc.—and opening the door for many to seek the help they need. Journalist Charles Sykes, however, is concerned that "we, as a nation, have developed an allergy to dealing with rather old-fashioned notions like personal responsibility. But you bring this up, and people look at you like you've been beamed in from the 19th Century."[8]

True, but then no one ever said that taking a stand that promotes personal responsibility and accountability would be easy or popular. But without the acceptance of personal responsibility, there will never be any lasting healing, regardless of how many self-help/recovery groups one might attend.

And that brings us to our position on the subject. Although any movement that truly helps and heals people—including psychological counseling and the self-help/recovery movement—has a measure of validity, every individual eventually must acknowledge his or her own responsibility and accountability before God.

Until that happens, we are locked into a position of rebellion against God. This is true not only in our own lives, but in the lives of our children. We have written this book around this concept to help hurting parents come to that place of healing for themselves, as well as to provide both practical and spiritual suggestions so that those same parents can also help bring their children from rebellion to accountability and healing.

Chapter 1

Understanding Our Children

❖ Fifteen-year-old Jeanelle was in tears. Her mother simply did not understand her. Why couldn't she have a mother like Terri's or Jackie's or Linda's? Their moms were cool. Unlike Jeanelle, her friends were allowed to date, and they didn't have to worry about things like curfews or having their activities screened or getting grounded for smoking or skipping school. In fact, Jackie's mom had given her birth control pills when she was thirteen, while Linda's mom had told her daughter that if she ever got pregnant to let her know and she'd help her get an abortion. So why did Jeanelle have to get stuck with a mom that was so old-fashioned?

Although teenagers have traditionally considered their parents old-fashioned to some degree, our children live in a world vastly different from the one in which their parents were raised. They face previously unheard of pressures and temptations. And, aside from the influence of the church and those homes which still strive to honor God, the biblical standards for right and wrong have nearly vanished from our land. In the midst of this moral vacuum with its damaging effects, young people have to deal with the normal coming-of-age problems, such as overactive hormones, peer pressure, and the desire to declare their own independence. No wonder they are vulnerable to the enemy of their souls!

Normal and Abnormal Behavior

In the introduction to this book, we listed some frightening statistics about teens, such as high rate of sexual activity, pregnancies, abortions, sexually transmitted diseases, criminal activity, etc. This was not done as a scare tactic or simply a dramatic way to begin the book. We wanted to draw your attention to the problems facing our youth today. Never before have we seen statistics of this magnitude. And no matter how hard we try to rationalize that kids have always had problems and gotten into trouble to one degree or another, we cannot excuse or justify the monumental rise in this sort of rebellious behavior.

Put simply, the problem is much more than normal "growing pains." However, before getting into defining just what the problem is, let us first clarify what it is not. To do so we need to differentiate between normal and abnormal behavior, between those children who are in rebellion and those who are simply going through that difficult "breaking away" process between childhood and adulthood.

Normal	Abnormal
1. Your child wants his or her curfew extended to that of his or her friends.	1. Your child ignores curfews, sometimes staying out all night.
2. Your child exhibits mood swings but is not violent or destructive.	2. Your child's mood swings are becoming more and more irrational and violent.
3. Your child shows less interest in family activities.	3. Your child has withdrawn from the family entirely, except for using the home as a "bed and breakfast."
4. Your child shows some impatience with family rules and restrictions.	4. Your child not only disobeys you but also speaks disrespectfully to you, even verbally abusing you.
5. Your child asks for what, at times, seems an excessive amount of money for personal expenses.	5. Your child steals money from you.
6. Your child's interests, activities, and/or friends show a gradual change.	6. Your child drops all former interests, activities, and/or friends.
7. Your child has an occasional difficulty at school.	7. Your child's grades, school behavior, and attendance drop suddenly.
8. Your child doesn't confide in you as often as before.	8. Your child becomes sneaky and secretive, even dishonest and manipulative.

3

Normal	Abnormal
9. Your child asks to dress in a popular style of which you do not approve.	9. Your child dresses in such a way that he or she knows will shock and offend you.
10. Your child shows an interest in music or movies of which you do not approve.	10. Your child defiantly listens to music with offensive lyrics, playing it as loudly as possible.

All children—regardless of personality, talents, interests, peer pressure, family situations, goals, dreams, aspirations, financial status, or racial background—must at some point go through a "normal" breaking away from their family. At times, their efforts to do so may be a bit awkward and possibly less than pleasant for those around them. And yet, their not going through this process would be abnormal. Actually, parents' childrearing techniques to this point should have prepared their offspring to spread their wings and begin to leave the nest a little at a time. Parents are to support and encourage their children as they make this important break.

However, this breaking away process can become a destructive force, not only in the life of the child involved, but in the life of the entire family. When this happens, the child's behavior can no longer be considered normal. Normal behavior is not exemplified by a spirit of rebellion or defiance. A child who is openly belligerent and disrespectful, who blatantly disregards the rules of the household as well as the feelings of those who live there, exhibits abnormal or rebellious behavior. Although this abnormal behavior is not necessarily an indication of satanic influence, we must be willing to at least consider that possibility.

At the same time, before assuming satanic influence in the child's behavior, we must consider other possibilities that might contribute to the behavior. For instance, we need to check for physical problems, such as an attention deficit disorder. It is amazing how many children, previously thought to be unmanageable, suddenly become model kids, as well as model students, when treated for this common disorder.

Just as the Bible teaches that certain illnesses and infirmities are related to demonic influence, it also teaches that many are not. However, even physical problems such as attention deficit disorders can be demonically induced. These situations require spiritual discernment and powerful intercessory prayer to solve the problem. Since the powers of darkness are more than ready to take advantage of physical and emotional weaknesses within an individual, parents need to be open to the fact that these situations could easily be a combination of both realms. Again, discernment and intercession are necessary for solving the problem.

Understanding Satan's role on earth is vital in learning to operate in that discernment and intercession. The Scriptures teach that there was war in heaven (see Rev. 12:7) and that Satan, an angel by the name of Lucifer, was cast out (see Rev. 12:9) because of his rebellious behavior. Now, he adds fuel to the fire of human rebellion, busily waging war on earth. Often our children are his primary targets. Because they are the future of society, they are under siege by this heavenly outcast, an enemy who is cunning, devious, clever— and deadly. He will use anything at his disposal to capture and hold them prisoner until, ultimately, they are no longer prisoners of war, but casualties.

A Destructive Culture

If we are to be of any help to our children in the midst of this escalating war, we must understand what they face in today's culture. What are the influences and pressures exerted upon them to yield to the enemy? What tactics does the enemy use to try to destroy them? How does he affect their minds to lead them into rebellion?

Most of the difficulties young people face come from changing ethics and morality. Satan has gained considerable control of our land by confusing right and wrong. Standards and principles of right living have fallen, one by one, until moral absolutes are nearly extinct. Situational ethics have become the accepted order of the day.

Principles of ethics and morality are primary protectors against the enemy of our soul. In the same way that speed limits protect us when we drive, God has set boundaries on our choices to keep us from hurting ourselves. When they are dismissed, the devil gains control, and he has no other plan than the complete destruction of that which God loves—humanity. In the midst of moral decay, we cross the lines of safety and do damage to ourselves mentally, physically, emotionally, and spiritually. Is it any wonder that our children are hurting? They search frantically for answers, only to become frustrated because there seemingly are none, and ultimately find themselves easy prey for the one who would incite them to rebellion. The answers they need involve moral absolutes. True God-given rights and wrongs offer protection and security, not bondage and fear.

Sadly, one of the devil's greatest assaults on our defenses has been made in the churches. Watered down versions of the Gospel are presented to people looking for social change from without, rather than personal change from within. When the truth of the Gospel is not proclaimed, there is no repentance, no new birth, no change, and no power. Dead religion prevails, and a living relationship with God is left by the wayside. There can be no other consequence but compromise. And so the devil gains one more easy access to the unprotected hearts and minds of our children.

Once the defenses of biblical principles and standards have been penetrated—in this case, nearly obliterated—the devil's purposes to steal, kill, and destroy go into high gear (see John 10:10). With nothing left to protect their souls, our children are exposed to music with demonic lyrics, which glorify drugs, perverted sex, violence, satanism, the occult, and even suicide. And, of course, much of the entertainment world has jumped on the devil's bandwagon, producing movies designed to convince our children that casual sex, drinking, drugs, and violence are viable lifestyles, practiced by the majority of the "successful and beautiful people."

As if all of that weren't enough, the enemy's influence is blatantly obvious even in school curriculum. You would have to look long and hard to find a schoolbook that depicts what a generation ago was considered a "typical" family—that of husband and wife, committed to each other in a lifelong relationship, seeking to raise their children according to God's standards. Instead, books now abound with teachings that deify humanity, reinforce the concept of situational ethics over moral absolutes, and portray "alternate lifestyles" as the norm, rather than as the destructive perversions they are referred to as in the Bible. If God is mentioned at all, it is usually in reference to some ancient religion that worships creation rather than the Creator.

If you doubt the power of these influences on young children, consider Elsa. Born and raised in pre-Nazi Germany, Elsa grew up in a school that taught the superiority of the white race, as well as total allegiance to Hitler and the fatherland. She was so indoctrinated in this thinking that, even as World War II drew to a close and the Allied soldiers were marching through the streets of her hometown, Elsa was convinced that it was all part of Hitler's plan and that, eventually, the tide would turn once again and Germany would triumph. Elsa was deceived, much like our generation today.

From our perspective, we can look back and wonder: How could anyone buy into Hitler's hateful master plan? At the same time, thirty or forty years ago, who would have believed that almost an entire generation could be plunged into such a deceitful and destructive lifestyle as the one now practiced by many of our children—lifestyles where pre-marital sex, drugs, and alcohol abound? Certainly this is not the case with every young person today; there are still millions of non-rebellious kids in the United States. Unfortunately, there are also large numbers involved in extreme rebellion.

All of this has happened because, a long time ago, the enemy began feeding lies into our own minds, the minds of those who would become parents of the current generation. Breaking down moral convictions and truths laid the groundwork for easy indoctrination of our children into rebellion as a way of life.

A Need for Acceptance

And now that way of life is reinforced and even applauded everywhere they turn. Not only do our children face problems and stress from ungodly, anti-family propaganda through music, TV, movies, and school, they are also caught in that difficult transition time between childhood and adulthood when peer approval is tantamount to success and happiness in life. One of adolescents' greatest needs is acceptance and friendship, a feeling of "fitting in" and belonging. And some will, when necessary, compromise their own values in order to meet this need.

If their friends tell them drugs are "cool," they will find it very difficult to remember that their parents have told them otherwise. When their best friends admit to, or even brag about, having sex, they're going to have a real tough time standing strong on any advice or conviction to remain pure until marriage. Because of a teenager's powerful need for acceptance, particularly among peers, the opposite of that acceptance—rejection—devastates the already insecure young person and leaves him or her wide open to enemy attack.

Everyone—including and especially teenagers—needs to feel wanted and to feel a part of a much bigger whole. This need is so central to our very beings that much of what we do in life revolves around fulfilling that need. Many emotional problems stem from this need going unfulfilled. To feel rejected and then to try to make it on our own is a sure way to escalate emotional problems. We simply weren't made to be independent of others.

As our body needs food for existence, likewise our soul needs acceptance. It determines its significance on the basis of the way we think others perceive us. Foundational to who we are, or at least who we believe we are, is our ability to see ourselves in relationship to others. Just being at peace with family members provides a great deal of emotional stability.

The more people we get along with in places around us like school, work, neighborhood, church, etc., the more fulfilling life becomes.

Immature people of any age cannot understand this. They are so wrapped up in thinking of "self" that they give the enemy an easy foothold to feed his lies into their minds: "No one cares about you"; "You're no good"; "You're a loser"; "You'd better defend yourself because everyone's against you."

We all do things in an effort to gain acceptance, and teenagers are no different. There is such a powerful need to be approved by others that we often go to unreasonable extremes to be recognized. Never is that more evident than during the teenage years, when children are moving into adulthood, trying to find their place and reason for being. This is why peer pressure can push a child in a negative direction, even when that child has been raised in a positive situation.

Of course, peer pressure affects more than just teenagers. But again, this occurs because the person being influenced has not yet discovered his or her identity and value through a relationship with Jesus Christ.

A Different Time

There is no question that young people, and especially teenagers, are hurting. Abused and neglected children are a major social problem. Peer pressure is stronger than ever before. Young people today are forced to grow up so fast that most of them cannot enjoy the normal pleasures of childhood. Back in the fifties and sixties, serious problems with teenagers involved drinking, fast driving, and poor grades in school. Today it is drugs, guns, gangs, and wholesale promiscuity, sometimes with occultic overtones.

Whereas thirty years ago teenagers were most likely to get into trouble, today elementary school students do so as well. Children as young as ten years of age are sometimes involved in gangs and some of them are even sexually active. It is hard to imagine a ten year old involved in drugs, gangs, and sex, but today's culture gives support to that kind of lifestyle.

Why are the young people of America having so many problems? Television, movies, and music pump the daily message into our children's minds that to be a success in life, they must drink a certain type of beer, wear a certain type of clothes, style their hair a certain way, have flawless skin, a "perfect 10" body, and drive a car that "makes a statement." Most kids look at these unrealistic images and realize they have lost the race before they start. Life has rejected them without even giving them a chance.

When young people are in that state of mind, the devil meets little resistance in leading these lonely, rejected children into destructive relationships with other lonely, rejected individuals. When success seems out of reach, it is easy to adopt the theory that "misery loves company." The next step, moving on to pain-killing substances such as alcohol or drugs comes all too easily. Even suicide becomes an option.

But are there other reasons for the problems children face? Some psychologists will tell you it all reverts to their parents. But what about the effects of a humanistic movement that deemphasizes God, family, morality, and accountability, while at the same time suggesting that most troubled people are victims of someone else's actions, reinforcing their belief that they have a right to their rebellion? Contrary to some counsel, no one has a right to rebel and cause hurt to other people. What possible right does a person have to be irresponsible, to be negligent, or to be dishonest because he or she has been victimized and is therefore operating out of pain? What may, to a degree, be understandable behavior because of influence from someone else does not constitute a right or an excuse to continue in that behavior. Certainly hurting people need society's help and understanding, but they must never be made to feel that unacceptable behavior is justified because at some point in the past they were wronged.

Frank Pittman, an Atlanta psychiatrist, puts it this way: "The adult child movement, by declaring practically everyone to be a victim of imperfect parenting and therefore eligible for lifelong, self-absorbed irresponsibility, has trivialized real suffering and made psychic invalids of those who once had a bad day."[1]

The self-absorbed victim mentality to which Dr. Pittman refers opens a door for the enemy of our soul. The Scripture says, "He who does what is sinful is of the devil" (1 John 3:8). Demonic influence works easily in people who have society's help in justifying any action that is wrong.

Ironically young people often say, "I just want to be different." Deep down, they truly do want to establish their individuality, but the fear that their own individual self-worth is not good enough prevents them from doing so. Instead, they "declare their independence" and individuality by dressing and looking like other insecure young people, banding together with them in a vain attempt to fulfill their need for love and acceptance.

Since the world is obviously not going to help our children find that love and acceptance, it is absolutely vital that we parents model a life of love, acceptance, and forgiveness. This does not mean we allow an illegal or immoral lifestyle in order to accept them, but it does mean we love and accept each of our children as the unique individuals God intends them to be.

Times have indeed changed, but, deep down, people have not. The need for love and acceptance has always been a driving force within us, just as fear of rejection has always been a factor in making poor choices. But people are still the same in a lot of other ways as well. For instance, the fact that more teens are sexually active today does not necessarily mean that those past generations who weren't sexually active were "better" people. It simply means that today's youth are readily faced with many more temptations and opportunities than we were, and, in addition, they have been taught that yielding to those temptations is their "right."

Peer pressure today pushes vulnerable, acceptance-hungry young people to give in to temptations, at times rewarding them when they do. Past generations would instead have been snubbed by their peers for getting involved in these same activities. James Dobson recalled his own experience in his book, _Parenting Isn't for Cowards:_

> I attended high school during the "Happy Days" of the 1950s, and I never saw or even heard of anyone taking an illegal drug. . . . Some of the other students liked to get drunk, but alcohol was not a big deal in my social environment. Virginity was still in style for males and females. Most of my friends respected their parents, went to church on Sunday, studied hard enough to get by and lived a fairly clean life. There were exceptions, of course, but this was the norm. It is no wonder that my parents were concentrating on other anxieties.[2]

Sounds good, doesn't it? That is the kind of world we would like to be raising our own kids in. But we are not. As we said, people may not have changed, but the world has. "Happy Days" is a TV program, portraying what life was like when some defenses were still in place to protect our lifestyle and that of our children from the encroachment of the enemy. But since that era, those defenses have been crumbling faster than we could ever have imagined, and the enemy has been successful in his attempts at breaking through those crumbling defenses to get to our children.

Now, many of our young people are consorting with the enemy, although few of them are doing so knowingly. Therefore we must understand our children—what is normal behavior and what is not—so that we can help them break free from the one who has come to capture and destroy them.

Chapter 2

The Shock

❖ Remember for a moment your first experience of looking at that beautiful baby. Hold again its tiny little hand. Marvel once more at its ability to sleep soundly in a world filled with unfamiliar noises. Breathe the fragrance of baby skin as you remember your kiss against that tender cheek. Feel the softness of blankets doing their best to replace the warmth of the womb.

It would have been morbid, perhaps even insane, to have thought that someday that child might become an alcoholic, a drug addict, or a prostitute. On the contrary, you believed your child would grow up to be admired and respected. Maybe he or she would become a doctor, a lawyer, or a schoolteacher. Maybe you saw your child destined to become a great leader.

We all want the best for our children and, in many

ways, have the best intentions of seeing that they get good things. The idealisms flow much easier when the child is still in the crib, and we can hold and love that child without the threat of back talk or the challenging of our authority.

Somewhere between this time of wonderful innocence in tiny pajamas and semi-adulthood, however, a child is really born. Millions of bits and pieces of information stored in the human mind will determine the kind of individual that he or she will become. And we parents will put a major amount of that information into those memory banks.

So we begin. "Did you hear that? He said da-da." "Honey, grab the camera, she's about to take her first step." "Will you look at this? Our boy is going to be a straight-A student. Look at all these pluses." "I'm sorry, Shirley, we'll have to go shopping together later; Jimmy's got Little League tonight." "You're so right, Jane, they certainly do grow up fast. I bought Julie her first bra last Saturday."

And finally, "He's been arrested for what?"

Nothing prepares us for that first mind-boggling realization that our child has become involved in something illegal or immoral. The shock slaps us in the face with such intensity that we wonder if we will ever stop reeling long enough to get our bearings again. And in the midst of it all, we ask ourselves countless times, *How can this be true?* And, *How could I not have known?*

RAY'S STORY_____

Dan sat stunned on the couch in my living room. His fourteen-year-old daughter was pregnant. It had been some years since I felt something similar to his devastation. But in spite of the fact that time does heal, at least to some degree, I still have flashbacks and momentarily feel the old pain.

As I listened to Dan, however, I experienced more than just a momentary flashback. It was as if I were transported back to the place in time where the shock first hit me full in the face—my daughter was gone. She had not come home and we had no idea where she was or even how she was. That moment of initial shock is almost beyond description, but it is never buried so deep as to be past reliving.

As Dan and I talked, I wrestled with what felt like the reopening of my own old wound. It hurt to listen. If I had not already been through this, I'm sure I would have been full of wonderful advice. Thankfully, I was not. I simply sat and listened—and hurt. It is a strange way to share one another's burdens, but at times, it's the only way.

_____ ◆

KATHI'S STORY_____

As overseer of a parent support group, I have learned that same truth time and time again. Parents come to the group in various stages of pain, but most, at some point, have experienced that initial shock and disbelief that temporarily numbed them from the agonizing heartache that was sure to follow. I know all too well the feelings experienced by these people.

When my son Chris began to exhibit what was obviously more than the normal teenage move toward independence, my husband, Larry, and I were concerned. But denial prevented us from recognizing and admitting that his behavior had indeed crossed the line from that normal teenage breaking away, as discussed in the previous chapter, to abnormal behavior, totally self-absorbed and impervious to the pain he inflicted upon others. As his attitude and behavior continued to deteriorate, we were finally forced past our denial into the shocking realization that our son was no longer only an innocent young boy being influenced by a negative peer group; he had indeed become a part of that negative influence. He had become a child with whom, if he were not ours, we would not want our own children to associate.

◆

Immediate Reaction

The immediate goal for most parents at that initial point of shock should be to find support, first through prayer and then through friends who will pray or simply listen. They can be a great help, particularly if they've been in similar situations and have managed to make it through to the other side.

But even when prayer support or a friendly shoulder is available, parents may still try to deal with the situation alone. Fear, guilt, shame, and continued denial can prevent parents from seeking the help they so desperately need to rescue their rebellious and often self-destructive teenager.

Trying to go it alone, however, is a bit like the little Dutch boy trying to plug up the hole in the dike: You may be able to hold back the tide for a time, but eventually the pressure is going to build to the point of rupture. Then the flood will come rushing in, leaving destruction and devastation in its wake. At that point, you may find that more than your teenager has been destroyed. Your entire family will undoubtedly have been affected, and the damage may be beyond repair.

There is much to consider when this sort of shock hits. First and foremost, again, is to seek God through prayer. As we said earlier, prayer is our first line of defense, because without God, all other help is useless. Second, sound biblical counsel is vital. You may very well be up against demonic forces that will not succumb to the advice of the world—advice that is not biblically based. Third, if possible, find a trusted, established support system, whether it be your own friends and family, your church, or a parent support group. And, fourth, be sure you have gathered together as many facts about the situation as possible _before_ plotting any long-term strategies.

For instance, suppose your child's grades have suddenly plummeted at school, he or she has lost all interest in extracurricular activities, has begun to associate with an entirely different set of friends, is experiencing wild mood swings, and is becoming virtually impossible to live with. It would be foolish to try to treat the situation without first gathering all the pertinent facts. Hiring a tutor to help your child study, monitoring the child's friends, or trying to calm your child when he or she is in the midst of a violent tantrum is useless if, in all probability, your child has a drug problem.

Get a Proper Perspective

Your support system can be more objective than you about the situation and can help you ascertain if, indeed, there is drug involvement and how best to go about getting your child help before the problem worsens. Does your child need to be involved in a residential drug program such as Teen Challenge or would outpatient counseling be sufficient? Do you and your family need to get involved in a group that will educate you about drug abuse and teach you how best to help your child become drug free? Which programs treat the spiritual dimensions of addictive problems, and which limit themselves to the physical and emotional aspects? These long-term strategies must be considered carefully and with much wise counsel before any decisions are made.

You will also find that others can help you gain a proper perspective on the problem. You may tend to overreact and need a more balanced viewpoint, one that says, "It's not time to act until assumptions have been validated." Or, if you tend to underreact, someone may need to tell you, "Get moving before you lose anymore ground!"

Of course, if the situation calls for short-term, life-saving measures, do whatever is necessary to quell the immediate crisis. In other words, put out the fire before you start investigating the fire's origin. If your child is suicidal, take the steps to ensure his or her safety. Discovering and dealing with the causes leading up to the suicidal condition will take time anyway, so concentrate your initial time and energy on saving your child's life. The process of unraveling and healing the problems will come later.

Whatever you do, don't let the shock drive you into isolation. This is the worst possible course of action you can take, particularly if the problem is a spiritual one. The devil knows there is strength in unity, so he is determined to keep you fighting this battle alone. After all, it makes his job much easier.

Please remember that, although you are still in shock and having a hard time believing what has happened, you have just been thrust into a life-or-death battle. Call for reinforcements! The stakes are too high to allow yourself to be intimidated by the question, "What will people think?" Besides, other parents who have been in your situation will confirm that most people respond by saying, "How can I help?" And even if you do get a negative reaction or two—

anything from a raised eyebrow or a lecture on how to raise problem-free children or even a shunned relationship—is your child not worth the risk?

Ed felt so ashamed about his daughter's association with drugs and her generally rebellious lifestyle that he did not want anyone to know about it. For months he kept silent until finally he couldn't keep it inside any longer. Opening up about his problem for the first time, he poured out his heart to a small group of trusted friends—the ones he had been so hesitant to tell—only to find that they immediately rallied to his side. In describing that experience, he later said that he felt as if a great weight had fallen off his shoulders. There was tremendous relief in not having to protect some sort of self-image.

If your child were dying of an incurable disease, would you not gladly give your own life to save his or hers? Of course you would. We must understand then, even in the foggy midst of shock, that rebellion is no different from cancer. If left unchecked, it can kill your child as surely as any other deadly disease.

Therefore, as numbing as the shock may be, we must resolve to take the necessary steps to save our children's lives. Step number one is to seek help—through prayer, through biblical counsel, through establishing a trusted support system.

Once you've done that, the other steps, as difficult as they may be, will fall into place.

Chapter 3

The Pain

❖ Ron was so dismayed over the painful difficulties of life, including those of his rebellious son, that he wanted to run away. One day, while driving, he had an almost overwhelming urge to keep going right on out of town and not look back. Only the realization of what he would be doing to those he left behind kept him from making such a tragic decision.

All it takes is a series of devastating experiences, and pain begins to slink about like a panther in the forest. It is not always on the attack, but it lurks in the shadows with its eerie and frightening presence. The phone rings late at night and you jump, wondering if you are about to be pounced upon again. When you feel good, you are afraid to enjoy it because you know that someday you will not feel good again, and you live in dread of that day. Presently, things may not look good. But time teaches that things do get better. We do get past the problem. And, for the most part, we get past the pain. Things have a way of looking different after the shock and disappointment of a difficult situation wear off. The important thing is not to become discouraged and give up when, like Ron, the pain becomes so overwhelming you want to run away from it all.

The Emotional Response

When a problem comes, emotions usually rise to the surface immediately. They drive us to try to get rid of the emergency as quickly as possible, which basically amounts to putting temporary bandages on the problem. We then have a false sense of accomplishment, when, in actuality, we have done nothing at all. In fact, at times like these, our judgments only make things worse. Anxiety and fear press on the accelerator of our feelings, spinning our wheels deeper into the sands of depression and despair.

Brian was caught shoplifting and had to face the consequences in court. His father, a trusted pastor, could not believe what was happening. When Brian finally spoke his mind, he expressed his resentment at having continually been told over the years that they were short on money. Brian's father had counted it a joy to work for the Lord without a grand salary and the security of financial gain. He, by no means, had reveled in his sacrifice, but he had accepted it with a certain amount of contentment, knowing that this world's goods cannot buy the presence of the Lord. Brian, on the other hand, had not yet met God on those terms and, to him, God was the reason they were living in semi-poverty.

Hold steady, Dad. Take a deep breath. What you do next is critical. Don't react too fast. Of course, all of that's easy to say; however, Brian's dad is still human and he must face parishioners as well as townsfolk. And no matter what happens, someone is bound to misunderstand. Because whether we like it or not, our children's actions cast reflections on us. Brian will be all right and so will his father. But only because many who are involved recognize the greatest need is not found in addressing what people choose to think, but in directing true love to a confused young man. With the right amount of understanding, Brian will eventually make his parents proud.

Emotionally-oriented blame rushes to solve the problem by pointing fingers in every direction. It usually does so without full examination of the facts. Brian needs correction. Yelling at him or criticizing and condemning him is not the solution. If Brian is belittled in this situation, the problem will most likely get worse before it gets better.

Wrong should never be arbitrarily covered up. Recognition of the error, along with proper accountability, is the only way to true healing. Look first at the situation with restoration in mind, rather than faultfinding, and mountains of additional pain will be avoided—as

27

Brian's father discovered as he began to deal with his son's problems out of love rather than condemnation. Although Brian's situation called for spiritual warfare—since the enemy was playing on Brian's weaknesses in an effort to lure him into illegal behavior—it was love, born out of understanding for Brian's behavior, that enabled his father to draw Brian back and to defeat the devil in his attempt to destroy the boy.

Blame and Guilt

When children first show signs of rebellion—meaning any sort of behavior that blatantly refuses to accept or submit to reasonable authority, particularly parental authority—it is not unusual to blame the child for the problem. Anger burns as we question how our children can do this to their own family. Soon the blame may shift, however, as parents frequently begin to blame each other. How easy to see numbers of things our spouse did or failed to do as a good parent. But, eventually, the pain of blame is usually turned inward.

If blame represents the bullets we shoot at each other and at ourselves in an attempt to deal with the problem, condemnation, with its deep dimensions of guilt, is the devastation when the bullet strikes home. True guilt is much easier to deal with, but much if not most of what we find at hand is false guilt, the kind that provides no solution. This kind of guilt has but one purpose and that is to destroy. It crushes the emotions, creates anxiety, and destroys any confidence that we can ever be whole or worthwhile again.

Owning up to any part of the problem for which we should take responsibility is not easy. But neither is dealing with guilt. Blasts of accusations knock us emotionally off our feet. And they knock others down as well. Eventually, it seems impossible to get up and life feels useless.

Our children can add to these pressures so much that we feel overwhelmed. When things get tough, we are tempted to seek one more fun-filled fling in life before blazing out into eternity. But what about the mess we leave behind? What about the pain generated in other lives?

John became discouraged as trouble developed between him and some of his children. One Sunday morning, as the family drove into the church parking lot and up to the front door where he would drop them off, John collapsed emotionally. He pulled away as if he were going to park the car and join them in a few moments, but instead he headed for the exit. As he sat ready to turn back onto the roadway, he realized that if he made that decision, he would never return.

John took quite a while trying to make up his mind. Finally, he put the car in reverse and joined his family. Who knows how much might have been lost had he not turned around? It has taken a long time, but recently one of those wayward children has decided that he needs the Lord, a decision he might never have made had his dad decided to leave.

The most important thing in these situations is to hold onto your faith and believe that your children will eventually be free of their destructive lifestyles and join you in your faith. Keep holding on, no matter how bleak the circumstances. Above all, don't be too proud to ask for help. It's a lot easier to hold on when you have someone holding with you.

RAY'S STORY

When Ralyn's rebellion left my heart crushed in tiny little pieces, I would share my pain with someone who would hold my special circumstance before the throne of God. These people may be hard to find, but I guarantee you, they are there.

It took years after our problems with Ralyn started before things began to turn around. Our negative, anti-authority daughter, however, became much more temperate in her behavior. Communication lines once again opened, and we began to make progress in the healing of our relationship. Without question, I believe this came about because people prayed, because I prayed. How long do you pray? You never stop. Even when your children return, you continue to cover them in prayer, learning that prayer is not only asking God to help, it is also doing violence against the enemy whose influence fuels our children's rebellion.

◆

*KATHI'S STORY*_____

I feel it is absolutely necessary to continue in prayer for our children—and to make those rebellious ones aware of our prayers on their behalf. Although Chris still sees the world as much more inviting than serving the Lord, he has never turned down my offers to pray for him. In fact, when he is up against something that, to him, seems overwhelming, he will approach me and ask me to pray for him.

Knowing that I cover him in prayer daily is a comfort to him, even and especially in the midst of his rebellious lifestyle. I firmly believe it is a constant reminder to him of God's call upon his life, a call I am confident he will someday answer. Until then—and even after that—I will never cease to pray for this son whom God has entrusted to my care.

_____ ♦

The Experience of Pain

Certainly there will be days, even weeks and months, when you find you cannot pray. Yet when your heart continues to cry to the Lord, that's prayer too. Let it weep from within, but also let God comfort you in your sorrow. One parent shared how she was comforted just realizing that even God has rebellious kids. Adam and Eve were a disappointment to Him.

Some parents have waited a long time to see a child restored. Their children are far past their teenage years and are still living in rebellion. Don't give up!

In the meantime, you'll continue to feel the pain. It won't be easy. Some of that pain will come directly from those tiny little hands and tender little lips that aren't so tiny and tender any longer, those children that you brought into the world and loved and nurtured and for whom you had such great dreams, and who have now seemingly dashed those dreams with their destructive behavior.

Some of that pain will come out of nowhere and, when you least expect it, will reopen your wound. The best intentioned people are often a source of this extended pain. It is surprising how the testimony of someone whose pain has been healed can, at one moment, bring the hope that says, "Our miracle is just around the corner." And yet, at other times, the same testimony deepens our pain with tormenting jealousy. We cry silently, "Why do they rejoice and I'm still in pain?" It is even worse when we rub shoulders with those parents whose kids became model citizens, those proud individuals who beam at the mention of their children's names.

The pain comes in other ways as well. Parents who already rejoice over promises God has given them in their heart concerning future restoration cause us to wonder why God has not spoken to us. Another parent may also rejoice as she lays the burden of her children before the Lord. "I've turned my children over to God," she smiles. "I know I can trust Him." You try to believe for that kind of faith, but it is not there. Crying helps a little, but how long can you cry? How long until you run out of tears?

And, of course, in the midst of our own pain, we must deal with the fact that, no matter how rebellious and hardened our children may have become, they too are hurting—which only multiplies the pain already overwhelming us. But because we are parents, programmed by past actions to reach beyond our own pain in order to help our children, we try to do just that. And instead of appreciating our sacrifice, they reject our help, refusing even to see the pain crying out to them from our anguished hearts.

Rebellious teenagers do not seem to notice that their parents are hurting too. They are too wrapped up with trying to dull and deny their own pain through whatever means they can find—drugs, alcohol, or sex. They don't understand that their pain—whether caused by the everyday difficulties of growing up, attacks from the enemy, or their own rebellious behavior—has been reproduced in their parents. Young people think of their parents as invincible. Parents put bandages on pain, they don't feel anything. The truth of this is echoed in a common statement from teenage lips: "You just don't understand!"

The more deeply parents love their children, the more deeply they are hurt when defiance and disobedience find their way into the home. When Peggy discovered that her fifteen-year-old daughter was pregnant, her pain was so great you could almost reach out and touch it as she shared her findings that her daughter had been having sex for about a year.

Certainly, young people today are hurting, and they will hurt even worse if our society does not change. But we parents must acknowledge our own very real pain, a pain that is born out of deep love and concern for our children's welfare. We do not want to draw attention away from mistreated and abused children or to divide the issue of pain into two different camps; we simply feel that parents must admit their own intense suffering too. These same parents will never be able to effectively help their children until they receive help themselves and understand what is happening to them and to their children.

The pain experienced by both parents and children in the growing-up process can be intense. Let no one minimize that. And it can last a long, long time. But the good news is that, in spite of the pain, both can get through it. There is hope . . . and there is healing.

Chapter 4

What Happened?

❖ Marty and Kathryn had both become Christians soon after their marriage and had dedicated Robbie, their only child, to the Lord when he was one month old. They had raised him in church, being careful to set strong moral examples in their own lives and practicing a loving but firm parenting style throughout Robbie's growing up years.

Their first hint of trouble came during Robbie's adolescence, when he began to get in trouble at school. His grades plummeted and all the encouragement and tutoring his parents offered made no difference. Counseling in Robbie's early teens brought little response and evoked no positive change in his behavior. Marty and Kathryn's concerns increased, but when Robbie was arrested at sixteen for dealing drugs, they were devastated. Not even in their wildest fears had they imagined something like this!

For some of us, the shock and pain of discovering the depths of our children's rebellion slam into us with the force of a tidal wave, while the question, "What happened?" swirls through our minds like a hideous accusation. How can this be? Where did we go wrong? Why didn't we see it coming? What kind of parents are we that we could have allowed something like this to happen to our child?

We Are Deceived

Although the progressive devastation of rebellion has been with us since Adam and Eve, its scope and magnitude have intensified to horrifying proportions in the last three decades. For the most part, responsibility and accountability have become objects of scorn. Rebellion is not only accepted, it is also glorified. We have come to a place of calling good evil, and evil good. Those in open rebellion are seen by many as heroes, rather than criminals. As the apostle Paul describes it in Romans 1:32, "Although they know God's righteous decree that those who do such things deserve death, they not only continue to do these very things but also approve of those who practice them."

Which helps explain why many parents today have trouble identifying some of the early warning signs of abnormal rebellion within their children. What would have been considered totally unacceptable behavior in children thirty years ago has become the accepted norm today—because we have been programmed to believe a lie. Rebellion is viewed by many as a mere exercise of rights, rather than the blatant sin against God that it is. As Paul wrote the church at Rome:

> Everyone must submit himself to the governing authorities, for there is no authority except that which God has established. The authorities that exist have been established by God. Consequently, he who rebels against the authority is rebelling against what God has instituted, and those who do so will bring judgment on themselves.
>
> (Rom. 13:1–2)

No wonder it's so easy for our kids to deceive us— we've already been deceived into believing that rebellion is normal and acceptable.

Because of our own deception, it is difficult for us as parents to view our children objectively. Therefore, our first reaction to the discovery of the depth of their rebellion is often one of disbelief. That once amicable, respectable, loveable young person has suddenly become someone totally opposite. There is a stranger in the house and we can't wait for him to leave. And yet, at the same time, we cannot force ourselves to throw the intruder out because he's clothed in the body of the child we love.

If the rebellion persists for any length of time, hope and hopelessness compete frequently for our attention. We work hard to bring the situation under control and then, just when things start to look good again, disaster breaks loose. Back and forth we go between encouragement and discouragement, until we are mentally, physically, and emotionally drained. We try to take a vacation or find rest in some other way, but no matter what we do, thoughts constantly return to the situation, refusing to leave for any appreciable period of time. We can be shopping, working, mowing the lawn, washing dishes, celebrating a birthday—and when we least expect it, we suddenly are face-to-face with the problem.

The cares of life are so demanding that few people take stock of the early stages of teenage rebellion. It is easy to neglect the situation, either because we do not know what to look for or what to do, or because we hope it will soon pass. When it does not, stress is manifest in the entire family. Spouses blame each other. Guilt and shame court the emotions not only of parents but brothers and sisters as well.

We search our hearts, looking for answers. We turn to professional people—counselors, pastors, and doctors—but soon find that many of them are confused as well. We labor over advice and explanations, but we soon discover that even the professionals do not understand what is happening. They search for answers too. And, sadly, in far too many cases, their analysis is faulty. Many well-meaning secular counselors and even some misinformed or uneducated Christian counselors advise clients that rebellion is indeed normal, even healthy. Little counsel is given regarding the possibility of demonic activity or spiritual warfare. Even practical advice may be watered down.

Virginia wisely sought counsel in order to appropriately deal with her daughter's defiant, destructive behavior. Unfortunately, in her attempt to get help, she did not find wise counsel. Virginia was told that her daughter's rebellion was caused by Virginia's religious beliefs, which "stifled" her child's "creativity." According to the counselor, Virginia's "puritanical standards" were "detrimental" to her teenager's "proper sexual growth and personal fulfillment." Parenting is difficult enough without faulty advice like that!

Virginia then turned to her pastor who, although a born-again Christian who recognized the problem with rebellion in Virginia's home, had never been trained in the area of spiritual warfare and therefore had no idea how to counsel Virginia. Thankfully, Virginia finally found her way to a Christian counselor who was equipped to advise her both practically and spiritually, and she is now seeing progress with her daughter.

Wholesale blame for teenage rebellion, along with many adult emotional disorders, is being thrown on what is commonly called the dysfunctional family. Although we agree that there is validity in the term *dysfunctional* when applied to many of today's families, we are concerned that the term not become a catchall, improperly appropriated as an excuse for continuing in destructive and irresponsible behavior. Those looking for just such an excuse will eagerly latch on to the theory that their own problems are a result of their mother's or father's poor parenting skills.

In considering a client's dysfunctional family, a well-meaning counselor may say, "Your behavior is understandable because of what you've been through, but it is not excusable and you must learn to take responsibility for it." The client, however, may choose to hear, "You have a right to be dysfunctional. You have a right to have severe emotional problems, to feel low self-esteem, to feel rejected, hurt, bitter, angry, and resentful. Your problems are not your fault. They're your parents.'" Any hint of the need to accept responsibility for one's actions is immediately rejected by anyone operating out of a spirit of rebellion or defiance.

If most of the emotional problems faced by people today were solely the result of dysfunctional families, then why is not everyone in the family dysfunctional? Often severe rebellion only strikes one or two of the children. The others go on to be relatively free of it.

Not Always Parental Neglect

Young people rebel from every walk of life. Race, color, creed, socio-economic status make no difference. They rebel in every kind of home environment. Good homes and bad homes (and there truly are dysfunctional homes, homes that contain a disproportionate amount of deviate behavior), are affected by a rebellion that can only be described as a phenomenon.

To say that when a child goes wrong it is entirely the fault of the family is simplistic. To say that teenage rebellion is fundamentally the result of parental neglect and abuse is unrealistic. Far too many parents raised their children well, and yet, when it was time for those same children to make choices, many of them chose irresponsible actions. The fact is that good homes can produce both good and bad kids, just as both good and bad kids can come from bad homes.

At the same time, while many of us who have tried to raise our children in healthy, loving homes continue to struggle with a rebellious teenager, the nonbelieving family across the street, where God is dishonored or ignored at best, have children who seemingly grow up problem-free. How can this be? Is there any benefit in having a good home?

Of course there is (see Deut. 7:9). God's Word is full of promises for the children of those who believe in and honor His Word. But those promises are not guarantees that a child will not rebel, especially since Satan is much more threatened by those children growing up in God-honoring homes, children whose lives have been dedicated to God's purposes. Is it not a logical conclusion that he will work that much harder to bring destruction upon children from Christian families than upon those from unbelieving homes where he feels victory is already assured? Therefore, those of us who know the truth must also practice it daily, modeling it to our children even as we intercede and intervene on their behalf, doing battle with all the forces that would feed and foster rebellion.

According to the Bible and contrary to the belief of some modern-day thinkers, rebellion is not normal. It isn't a natural part of growing up. We can't simply say, "Kids will be kids," when rebellion enters our home. Biblically, rebellion is related to witchcraft (see 1 Sam. 15:23) and is always punished severely (see Num. 16). The rebellion of Adam and Eve resulted in the separation between God and the entire human race. Only through the shedding of the blood of God's Son were the effects of rebellion quelled and the way opened for God and man to be reunited once again.

To believe that a certain amount of rebellion is normal is to believe that a certain amount of sin is normal. Sin and rebellion affect each of us, but that does not make them normal. God did not create man to live in sin or rebellion; as Christians, we must accept the fact that God's original creation is what's normal, not the distortion of that creation. There was no sin or rebellion in God's original design for the human race. Throughout the thousands of years since that time, God's view of sin and rebellion has not changed, since God Himself has not changed (see Heb. 13:8). Society may claim to have become enlightened and changed in the way they view things, but man's viewpoint is not to be accepted when it conflicts with the viewpoint of God Himself.

Rebellion is demonic, whether it is the rebellion of

Adam and Eve in the Garden of Eden, or the rebellion of teenagers who ignore parental authority when it conflicts with their own desires. As discussed in chapter 1, the destructive, rebellious behavior that accompanies the defiance of parental authority is not the same as the normal experience of growing up and breaking away from family.

Furthermore, we must not confuse rebellion with a child's legitimate attempts to break away from truly abusive situations. Although parents are called by God to lovingly discipline and raise their children according to biblical principles, that does not give them license to abuse their children in any way—physically, sexually, verbally, emotionally, or spiritually. Child abuse is a very real problem, and the principles outlined in this book should in no way be misinterpreted as permission to engage or continue in abusive practices. Jesus, in referring to children, warned that "if anyone causes one of these little ones who believe in me to sin, it would be better for him to have a large millstone hung around his neck and to be drowned in the depths of the sea" (Matt. 18:6). To misuse or abuse our parental rights and responsibilities is a grave offense, one for which we will someday answer to God Himself.

In dealing with rebellion, the final question is this: How much of this behavior will we allow? Every inch of allowed rebellion will be utilized to gain more ground.

Margaret learned that the hard way. Although she had a long-standing rule that cigarette smoking was not allowed in her home, when her strong-willed teenage son, Marty, openly broke that rule, she weakened and agreed to permit his smoking so long as he confined it to his room. It wasn't long, however, before Marty was smoking in the living room and at the kitchen table. Then one day, to Margaret's horror, he defiantly lit up a marijuana cigarette, daring her to stop him. What had begun as a matter of holding already established ground turned into a major battle, not only for regaining lost ground but for stopping any further encroachment on parental territory.

We believe any amount of rebellion is abnormal when seen in light of God's original design for humanity. True, children do reach an age where they begin to move from dependence on Mom and Dad to independence, and that's normal. However, that move can be made in a respectful manner, totally and completely apart from rebellion, and in full cooperation with wise parents who recognize and even encourage their growing children's need to make such a move.

Time and again, the Bible warns us to guard against being deceived. We are to walk in the Truth (Jesus), because that is how we are set free (see John 8:32; 14:6). Truth frees; deception enslaves. God desires our children to be set free, but that cannot happen until they come face-to-face with Truth, until they have a personal encounter with and make a personal commitment to Jesus Christ.

Satan, whom Jesus referred to as "the father of lies" (John 8:44), is the one "who deceives the whole world" (Rev. 12:9 NKJV). In this instance, "the whole world" refers to any and all who have not had that face-to-face encounter with and made that personal commitment to the One who is Truth, Jesus Christ Himself. But Satan is not satisfied with deceiving the whole world; his greatest aim is to "deceive even the elect" (Matt. 24:24)—the Church.

Believe the Truth

When Jesus shed His blood at Calvary to take away our sins and to open the door to restoration with the Father, Satan's arsenal of weapons was reduced to one—deception, the same weapon he used in the Garden of Eden prior to the Fall. And so he continues to use that weapon against the Church with a vengeance, for he sees it as his only hope to defeat the hated followers of the One who "disarmed" him and made him and his demonic hordes "a public spectacle . . . triumphing over them by the cross" (Col. 2:15). And if he can't get to us personally, then he will do his best to get to us through our children.

Without exception, when our children are in rebellion, they are also in the grips of deception. Which is all the more reason that we must "watch and pray" (Mark 14:38) and continue in the Truth if ever we are to see them set free. The price has already been paid for their freedom; now it's up to us to do everything within our power to lead them to receive it. This includes modeling an ongoing love-relationship with Jesus Christ, being consistent in raising our children according to biblical guidelines, both practically and spiritually, and seeking and walking in sound, moral counsel.

The important thing to remember here is that it is never too late. Many parents reading this book may be thinking, *I didn't know any of this when my children were little. I didn't have a relationship with God and, therefore, knew nothing about raising them according to biblical guidelines.*

Although the best cure for any problem is prevention—and we certainly encourage the instituting of God's principles and guidelines for childrearing from the moment of birth—we also want to encourage parents who, for whatever reason, did not do so. As we've already explained, even the best parenting techniques do not ensure that our children will not rebel. So no matter what parenting skills—or lack thereof—you may have practiced with your children to date, resolve now to relate to your children, whatever their age, in the way that our heavenly Father relates to us— with a mixture of firm discipline and lots of unconditional love.

By doing that, we no longer need torture ourselves with the "What happened?" question. Understanding the demonic roots of rebellion points us to God for the answers to the problems associated with that rebellion. As we seek Him, we can rest in God's many promises for our children, knowing that He loves them much more than we do, and that He is a God who can bring good even out of our failures (see Matt. 6:33; Rom. 8:28).

▼

Chapter 5

The Natural Side of the Problem

❖ Marcus was angry. He could not understand why he had been convicted of assault.

"All I did was punch the guy out," he explained. "I mean, it isn't like I killed him or anything. I've beat up guys worse than that before and never got locked up. Besides, this guy deserved it."

The guy Marcus was referring to was his high school math teacher, Mr. Dowling. When Marcus received a failing mark from Mr. Dowling, he had confronted the teacher with the fact that, without a passing grade in his class, Marcus would not graduate.

Mr. Dowling had tried to explain to Marcus that he couldn't possibly give him a passing grade since Marcus had seldom shown up for class, had done almost no homework, and had failed every exam the entire quarter. Although Mr. Dowling had warned Marcus several times that he was in danger of failing, Marcus had made no effort to improve his study habits. So when Mr. Dowling refused to change the failing grade, Marcus punched him in the face, breaking his nose and knocking out three teeth. Although the boy's attorney argued that, at the time of the confrontation, Marcus had been under the influence of drugs due to stress at home and therefore could not be held accountable for his actions, the judge sentenced Marcus to six months in a juvenile facility.

Marcus's belief that he should not be held accountable for his actions is, unfortunately, a belief held by many in society today. Marcus felt his behavior was justified because he saw Mr. Dowling as the cause of his problems. Marcus's attorney wanted the judge to believe that the assault should go unpunished because the boy had chosen to participate in another illegal activity—drug use—in an effort to escape stress at home.

This failure to accept responsibility for one's own actions and to understand that each of those actions will have a reaction or consequence is dangerously widespread, particularly in our youth. This belief system lends itself to demonic influence since lack of personal accountability runs counter to God's Word.

A Legacy of Rebellion

In chapter 4 we observed that the last three decades have seen an unprecedented explosion of rebellion in our land. Rebellion, in the natural, is lawlessness, and lawlessness has gained a whole new dimension in America. Social historian Fred Siegel says, "We have conducted a 30-year experiment in desublimation. Everyone gets to act out. There are no consequences. It's been a disaster."[1]

Although originally much of that lawlessness seemed born out of a reaction to the Vietnam conflict, the issue is much deeper. America was supposedly fighting for democratic freedom during that time, but internally she wasn't free herself. Deep within there were strife, discontentment, and disagreement. Dissatisfaction with government was a key issue, and the entire political system came into question. Government became known as the "system." *System*, that indefinable word that describes an individual or group who determines our destiny, but whom we really can't find to confront. It was the "they" of that phantom bunch who exist behind the walls of an invisible bureaucracy. Take thirty years of a people who are fed up with government and yet, at the same time, can't seem to do anything about it and you set the stage for widespread contempt for authority.

One of Satan's greatest tactics in his bid to destroy the human race is to defile government. Make government restrictive to the point of oppression, and people can be taught to rebel in the natural process of necessary resistance. Rebellion in one sense can be described as an evil way of resisting those things which are thought to be wrong. Raise a generation of children

51

on negativism toward authority and, by the time their children are ready to make decisions, you have a society in which people do what is right in their own eyes (see Judg. 21:25), just so long as they do not get caught.

Soon government cannot keep up with the lawlessness and either has to back off on its law enforcement or increase its number of jails. It usually winds up doing both. It reexamines its laws and cancels those opposed to the majority of the people. Sadly, it often does so simply by neglecting regulations which are considered archaic or unenforceable. At the same time, enough unacceptable lawlessness exists that government must increase its ability to contain certain kinds of lawbreakers. Incarceration is the answer, and so our prison population grows.

Try raising a child in a society that does not respect authority and soon the influence winds up in your own home. Try teaching your children morality in an amoral and immoral culture and, somewhere along the line, you will meet resistance. Eventually you will face a challenge to your own authority.

Ineffective Solutions

The solution for some people is to take their children out of the culture, to raise a high fence between them and the children of the world. Unfortunately, by themselves, many parents can't provide the education that allows their children to mature in all aspects of life. If they are not careful, parents can turn their children into social misfits who, when finally forced to rub shoulders with the rest of the world, do poorly. Some of these kids have itched so long to experience life like other people that, once they are free of parents, they go overboard in worldly participation. They don't know where the boundaries are, and before they find out, they have gone too far and are in serious trouble.

This is not meant as a slap at home schooling; overall, we're for the concept. But, on the other hand, isolationism can have deadly consequences when the home shelter produces unrealistic views of the world. The Scripture exhorts us to remember that we are *in* the world, even though we are not *of* the world (see John 17:14).

Children bond to each other especially as they start talking. If they find they can relate to other children in the world, they will bond to them. This is why dialogue in the home is so necessary. That dialogue needs to be done in a respectful manner, with parents listening as well as talking. Many parents consider a lecture to be the same as a dialogue, but a lecture is one person talking *at* another person, while a dialogue is two people talking and listening and sharing *with* each other. In addition, this dialogue needs to include practical applications of what God's Word has to say about certain situations, always expressed in love, never used to prove the parent's point in an argument.

Without this kind of dialogue in the home, our children are prime targets for negative peer influence, including gang membership. We are convinced that the high involvement among kids in gangs today is caused, in large part, by a need to identify with a unit, a "substitute family," as it were. And the loyalties within those substitute families run strong.

Some parents dream of escaping from all this negative influence to some out of the way place that is safe from seductive worldly pressures. But where? There is really nowhere to run. Besides, even parents in small towns have problems. Simply escaping the big cities is no guarantee of escaping negative influence on their children.

Other parents put their children in private schools to solve the problem. That is an expense that not everyone can afford, and it is not a cure-all. Even environments controlled better than the public school system can have a great deal of negative influence. Alcohol, drugs, and sexual promiscuity are still potential problems.

Many people would like to believe that Christian schools are the answer and, in some cases, they may be. However, Christian schools still contain some students who are not committed to the same lifestyle that you are—the same students who, in many cases, will negatively affect your children.

The Pull Toward Independence

Usually in the early teenage years children begin the move toward the independence that allows them to live lives of their own. As explained before, this move toward independence is normal; after all, adulthood is just around the corner. During this time, often somewhere around junior high, children are powerfully influenced to make adult decisions. Much of this influence will run counter to what you have tried to instill in them prior to this time.

These impressionable young people are confronted with the ethical and moral values of people around them, especially their friends, their peers. Television is no longer simply an attention-getting device that helps you keep track of your offspring. It is a powerful teaching tool that will affect the way they live for the rest of their lives. In reality, it introduces a kind of ethereal peer group. The sexy young lady in tight-fitting blue jeans represents their generation, as does the cool, muscular young man sauntering through the sand of the seashore. If Madison Avenue tells our kids they need something, they wind up believing they need it.

Having a peer group is a normal part of everyone's life, and is the first place a person recognizes his or her need for identity. Life, in a lot of ways, is really one great big "Who am I?" The group makes a person all the more conscious of this. Here young people see images of who and what they think they ought to be. Blurred as these images may be, they appear to offer fulfillment in life. They offer excitement, not to mention security, acceptance, and power.

Home life never did this, at least not in a way children could see. Home represents too much of a bland way of life in comparison to what the group has to offer. And, far too often home contains an atmosphere of hostility and bitterness. If you could step into the minds of one of your children for a moment, how do you think you would view the home in which you live? As humorist Josh Billings says, "Train up a child in the way he should go—and walk there yourself once in a while."

Home may also represent punishment and restriction. All homes need discipline, but some so wreak with it that anyone living there, whether young or old, experiences limitations suggestive of confinement. The very word *home* should suggest a place of comfort, a place a person wants to run to. Sadly, this isn't true for everyone.

Della was an only child whose father died before she was two. Although her mother never remarried, she lived with a succession of men, two of whom sexually molested Della before she ever reached her teens. By the time she was fourteen, she had opted for life on the streets. Twice, she was picked up by the authorities and returned home, where her mother's newest boyfriend beat her to "teach her a lesson." Della's mother stood by and said nothing. When Della was finally placed in a foster home just before her sixteenth birthday, she said it was the happiest she had ever been.

Although Della's case is extreme, it is not isolated. Countless children are beaten and abused daily by the very ones who should be their protectors. How tragic that children should be forced to run *from* their homes, rather than *to* them, for safety. And what a mandate to parents to create that place of safety and security within the home, rather than driving their children away through harsh and unloving distortions of their parental responsibilities.

Even in children raised in loving homes, however, the strong normal pull toward adulthood, now strengthened by the peer group, wrestles with parental strings yet to be severed. Some teenagers opt to cut them before the proper time, running away from home and often becoming stunted in their growth toward maturity. Others, however, realizing they are not yet equipped to support themselves, stay home and attempt to keep any unacceptable behavior hidden. If they are unsuccessful and their behavior is discovered, they may further compound the problem by lying.

At this point, parents often go into denial because they simply do not want to believe that their previously well-behaved child could have become involved in something illegal or immoral. These parents fail to understand that their child's attachments to a peer group and sometimes to a single individual can be so strong that the child is willing to sever all previous ties and moral commitments in order to maintain relationships with those peers.

Although it is heartbreaking to experience a child leaving home to pursue an illegal or immoral lifestyle, it is still extremely destructive for those whose children choose to remain in the home, becoming compulsive liars in an effort to hide their unacceptable behavior from their parents.

Darrel was both heartbroken and guilt-ridden because his fifteen-year-old daughter spent time in a rehabilitation center due to a recurring problem with drugs. Counseling at the center revealed that the girl suffered from very low self-esteem, which is common among those who become chemically dependent. The counselor also determined that her problem with low self-esteem worsened as a result of lying to her parents. Her opinion of herself continued to sink to an all-time low, which only added fuel to the fire of her drug addiction.

Eventually she admitted to taking drugs in an attempt to stop feeling bad, rather than to feel good. Darrel would be a vital part of his daughter's recovery, but he would first have to get past his own feelings of hurt and rejection before he would be any help to her.

Parents like Darrel who try to raise their children properly and give them the best they can afford will experience strong feelings of rejection when a child rebels. Personal rejection of love, as well as rejection of family moral values, deeply cut into former trust and respect. We are, to a large extent, what we think and what we believe. Our values and convictions are what make us who we are. These things determine our lifestyles. The food we eat, the cars we drive, the neighborhoods we live in, the church we attend—all represent who we are. When one of our children rejects any of these things, they, in effect, reject us. At least, that's the way we perceive it. And that hurts.

Unrealistic Expectations

The pain of rejection is often accompanied by another kind of pain called "unfulfilled expectations." We expect our children to make us happy by becoming what we want them to be. We expect them to carry on our strong religious and other personal convictions. We expect them to live our kind of lifestyle. And we expect them to be successful in everything. After all, we raised them to be this way.

Allowing ourselves to live in false expectations about our children and then passing those expectations on to our kids, either through verbal communication or simply by implied actions, is setting our families up for failure.

The Mauldings are a classic example. Michael and Joan Maulding had met in Bible college, where they both graduated with honors. Marrying soon after, their first child, Donna, was born slightly over a year later. By that time, Michael was pastoring a small but growing church, and Joan worked tirelessly as the faithful pastor's wife. Devoted to each other, Michael and Joan never entertained the slightest doubt but that Donna would grow up to be a model child and teenager, doing well in school and then going on to Bible college to prepare for some sort of full-time ministry before marrying and starting a family of her own. These expectations were conveyed to Donna both verbally and by implication.

Things seemed to go well during Donna's elementary school years, but soon after she hit junior high, her grades plummeted drastically. Michael and Joan were horrified when they met with a school counselor, who termed Donna's behavior as "classically boy-crazy." When Donna was confronted by both her parents and the counselor, she admitted not only to being interested in boys to the exclusion of her studies, but to having been sexually active since the age of twelve.

The shock waves that tore through the Maulding household left them all reeling. Only through wise counsel, combined with countless hours of prayer, Scripture reading, and communing with God, could this family understand the damage that had been done by their well-intentioned but unrealistic expectations—expectations which Donna felt she could never live up to, so why try.

Thankfully today, some fifteen years after the Maulding's discovery of their daughter's rebellious and promiscuous behavior, Donna has indeed fulfilled many of her parents' expectations. She is happily married to a fine Christian man, is expecting their first child, and is active in her church. But this portion of her parents' expectations was not fulfilled without their first experiencing a derailment of the falsehood that would say: Because I am a believer and am raising my children accordingly, they will not experience any of the problems of those children raised in non-Christian homes.

At the same time, it isn't just believers who can have unrealistic expectations for their children. What about the doctor or lawyer or businessman who assumes his child will follow in his footsteps, joining in the family practice or business, when in actuality the child has no interest in doing so?

Is it rebellion when the child follows his or her natural bent toward some other profession, rejecting parental blueprints for his or her life? When done in a respectful manner, certainly not. In fact, to be pressed into a mold formed for us by our parents when God has designed us for another purpose is to fail to fulfill our potential and to settle for a less than satisfying life. Parents, therefore, should encourage their children to seek and follow God's plan for their lives, whatever that may be.

Taking a Stand

Bringing our attitudes and expectations into line with what God's Word truly says about raising children is a major step in successfully defending our children from demonic influence. This may mean a radical change from the way we have thought or acted toward our children in the past. Several parent support groups have found that one of the most powerful and practical tools available to parents is that of changing the status quo in their homes and catching the children off guard with new ways of dealing with old problems.

If you have always reacted to your children in a certain way when they exhibit a certain behavior, change that reaction. Don't be so predictable! Your kids are used to pushing your buttons and getting a pre-programmed response. When they discover that you are no longer reacting to their button-pushing as expected, they will be forced to readjust their behavior, at least to some degree. It goes without saying that we cannot forcibly change someone else's behavior—including our children's—because everyone is born with a free will. But often we can influence change in others by changing our own behavior.

Ken and Anita had a son who sulked. Any time they would discipline him in any way, he would storm off to his room and slam his bedroom door until everything hanging on the walls rattled. At times he actually slammed the door so hard that things fell off the wall. Then he'd pout behind locked doors for hours.

In the past, his parents had reacted by pounding on his bedroom door and demanding that he open it. He ignored them, knowing they would get tired of pounding and yelling before he got tired of sitting in his room. Finally, at the suggestion of others in the support group, the parents informed their son that the next time he slammed his bedroom door and refused to come out, they would simply remove his door. Needless to say, that very announcement provoked a door-slamming episode. Immediately, his father went into the garage, got his tool kit, and removed the boy's door. They then informed him that he could earn his door back through good behavior. When he finally got it back, he was careful never to slam it again.

The daughter of another couple, Jim and Joyce, ran away from home every time she didn't get her own way. At first she would only stay gone a day or two, usually sleeping over at a friend's house. Soon, however, she was staying away for weeks at a time. The police would be alerted, but because the girl would eventually come home of her own free will without having been in any other legal trouble, the parents were at a loss to teach their daughter the consequences of her behavior. Any retribution on their part only resulted in another runaway episode.

And then someone in their parent support group suggested Jim and Joyce inform their daughter that should she run away again, they would simply sell her bed, assuming that she no longer needed it since she had chosen to live elsewhere. If and when she returned home, she would have to sleep on a sleeping bag on the floor.

True to their word, they did exactly that. Their daughter was incensed and demanded that they buy her a new bed, threatening to run away again if they refused. They did refuse, however, and assured her that her dresser and vanity would be the next thing to go. The girl has not run away since, and has only recently earned enough money through odd jobs to purchase a new bed for her room.

The obstacles to raising responsible, respectable children are many—and they are multiplying every day. As our world changes, so do the problems faced by our young people. That is why parents should be educated as to what their children are up against, and what can be done to counteract these obstacles.

Facing up to the fact that our children eventually are responsible for their own choices and must face the consequences of those choices, as well as refusing to get caught up in false expectations for their lives, is a good starting place. Understanding our children's accountability for their own actions keeps us from getting caught up in false guilt, guilt that Satan would gladly use to paralyze us into inaction.

Because he, after all, is the true enemy in this fierce war against our children. The next chapter will introduce you to this arch-enemy of families, as well as give you some guidance on how to successfully fight—and defeat—this very real foe.

Chapter 6

The Supernatural Side of the Problem

❖ Jodi's eyes blazed as she screamed at her mother, her diatribe peppered with obscenities. "I hate you!" she cried, her fist raised defiantly in the air. "And I hate your Jesus! I don't ever want to hear His name again, do you hear me? If you ever mention Him to me again, I'll . . . I'll kill you!"

Jodi's mother shuddered as she stared at the contorted face of her fifteen year old. In her heart, she knew that this was not her child, that she was up against demonic forces. Thankfully, she knew enough about spiritual warfare to take authority over the situation.

"You cannot kill me," she said calmly, speaking not to her daughter but to the controlling spirit. "I am a child of God. Jesus is my Savior and Lord, and you have no authority over me. I command you now, in the name of Jesus, to leave this house immediately." Jodi let out a bloodcurdling scream, then turned and ran out the front door. The demonic influence in Jodi's life was far from broken, but the immediate crisis had been averted.

Awareness of Demonic Activity

Twenty or thirty years ago the words "spiritual warfare" raised eyebrows—not to mention more than a few doubts—among many in America who questioned the validity of a supernatural realm that involved demons. Although the Bible describes in vivid detail an evil dimension lying just beyond our senses, those who couldn't see it often refused to believe that it was there. It was much easier to believe that, if demons did exist, they did so in primitive places, not in a civilized nation like our own.

Since that time, there has been a noticeable change in attitude toward this topic. People have realized that the spiritual climate in America is obviously affected by something sinister and beyond normal perception. Occultic activity has gained widespread interest. Exploring the "dark side" has become popular. The entertainment industry, with movies such as *The Exorcist* and *Poltergeist,* has capitalized on the work of demons, although they have made them look like mere Hollywood fantasy. Strange movie-like behavior, however, shows up on more than just the picture screen. Played out in far too many lives is a kind of bizarre behavior, not unlike Jodi's, that answers only to a realm beyond our senses. Something is all too real about this world that is supposed to be make-believe.

Almost everywhere you look there has been a tremendous increase of awareness in satanic activity. The news media reports stories of rituals, animal sacrifices, and possibly even human sacrifices. Today talk about demons does not surprise or alarm very many people. Most are not only aware of the realm but want to know more about it. Some seek information out of curiosity; others do so to guard against it. For more about this topic, ask a Christian bookstore for books on the subject; do not seek them out at a secular or new age bookstore, as the teachings may not be scriptural and could cause more harm than good. Seek the advice of a trusted pastor. Most importantly, pray for God's wisdom as you read your Bible for understanding, for He is the One who can best teach you about the demonic realm.

How much does this unseen diabolical spirit world really affect us? Paul Billheimer, author of *The Technique of Spiritual Warfare,* described it this way:

Humanity is beset by a host of self-conscious evil spirit personalities called demons, who are responsible for much, if not most, of the personality difficulties, complexities, spiritual pressures, and strains and the aggravated forms of evil that characterize our modern social order. . . . Any spiritual method or technique which ignores the presence and activity of these occult forces cannot possibly offer an adequate solution for the problems plaguing mankind.[1]

Those are pretty strong words, but totally in keeping with Scripture. Jesus lived in a society much like our own. And in it He cast out demons and delivered people from the enemy of their soul.

Satan, the instigator of the rebellion that led to the war in heaven, was cast out (Rev. 12:7–9). He had tried to usurp power that did not rightly belong to him, going so far that he actually thought he could eventually be "like the Most High" (Isa. 14:14). One of his ploys in trying to deceive humanity is to suggest that becoming like God is a possibility for everyone (see Gen. 3:5).

Although some controversy arises within the Church itself as to the specific characteristics and operations of demons, most Christian leaders agree that the devil and his demons do exist. They also agree that the devil was once an angel who, not content to serve God, chose to rebel and attempted to overthrow the throne of heaven. He persuaded as many angels as possible—one third, according to Revelation 12:4—to rebel with him. These rebellious angels who were cast out of heaven with the devil are referred to as "Satan's angels" or "demons."

When Jesus arrived on earth, the devil—that is, Satan—was in control (see John 12:31). Satan even approached Jesus, saying he would make Him number two in his worldwide plans if He (Jesus) would fall down and worship him (see Matt. 4:8–9). But Jesus gave him no ground because He had come to destroy Satan's works (see 1 John 3:8). God accomplished this task through Jesus on the cross and delivered us from the kingdom of darkness into the kingdom of His Son (see Col. 1:13). Whereas we were once a part of the enemy's kingdom (see Eph. 2:1–2), we have now been rescued (see 1 Peter 1:18–19) if we choose to appropriate the work that Christ did for us at Calvary.

"The devil made me do it" may not be an acceptable excuse for sinful behavior, but there may be more to the statement than most of us would like to believe. Jesus told Peter that Satan wanted to have him in order to sift him like wheat. It is interesting to note that, whereas Jesus could have stopped this encounter, He did not.

Instead, He told Peter He had already prayed for him that his faith would not fail. He further told him that when the sifting was over, he was to go on and "strengthen your brothers" (see Luke 22:31–32). Later, Peter wrote to the church describing Satan as a roaring lion going about seeking someone to devour (see 1 Peter 5:8). The apostle James also wrote about the enemy, recognizing that he must be resisted (see James 4:7), stressing also, however, that he can only be successfully resisted by those who have first submitted themselves to God. Paul was more specific: we do not wrestle against flesh and blood, but against principalities, against powers, against the rulers of darkness of this world, and against spiritual wickedness in high places (see Eph. 6:12).

Whatever you have believed in the past about this realm, you can presently find the same kind of satanic behavior that Jesus dealt with two thousand years ago. Sometimes you need go no further than one of your own children.

RAY'S STORY _____

I once sat in a meeting listening intently to the speaker when suddenly a piercing scream penetrated the auditorium. Later, in a side room where the young lady involved had been taken, I witnessed demonic activity firsthand. The words and attitudes that flowed from her mouth were without question the result of demons.

On a different occasion I saw yet another young lady under the same kind of influence. She writhed like a snake on the floor.

_____ ◆

KATHI'S STORY _____

One time I sat under a huge tent at a maximum se-curity prison in Texas, researching a book on spiritual revival within the prison system. At the end of the meeting, several counselors prayed and talked with inmates who wished to make commitments to Jesus Christ. One young man in his early twenties came forward hesitantly. I watched as, each time he attempted to step up to one of the counselors, he was seemingly stopped by an invisible hand.

Finally, a counselor close to him observed the man's

growing distress and laid his hand on his shoulder. Immediately the prisoner fell to the ground and screamed and hurled blasphemies and obscenities at the counselor. As the counselor knelt to the ground beside the writhing man, he spoke to the demon spirit: "In the name of Jesus Christ of Nazareth, I command you to release this man and come out of him now." The prisoner let out one last horrifying scream, and then relaxed. Soon he was crying like a baby, sobbing, "He's gone! He's gone! Oh, thank God, he's finally gone!"

Once free of the spirit that had controlled his life since his early teenage years, this young man gave his heart and life to Jesus Christ, and is now serving him faithfully in the prison chapel, using his own experience to minister to others in similar situations.

$\blacklozenge$

The Reality of Demons

In both lesser and greater degrees of influence, the enemy of our soul is wreaking havoc upon humanity, and especially upon the young people of our land. But not until it strikes close to home are we sometimes willing to look for answers that only Jesus can provide. His remarkable attack upon demons when He was here on earth, coupled with His words that all power both in heaven and on earth belongs to Him (see Matt. 28:18), becomes our only source of hope. He delivered one of the most discouraging statements a demon has ever heard. To His own, Jesus said, "I have given you authority to trample on snakes and scorpions and to overcome all the power of the enemy; nothing will harm you" (Luke 10:19).

As surprising as it may be to some, especially to those who recognize the reality of demon activity, not all warfare on behalf of our children involves supernatural confrontations with demons. Much of the warfare involves the simple teaching of basic biblical principles. What appears to be simply good parenting is often a great element of protecting our children from the evil one.

Evelyn is a Christian who has believed in spiritual warfare for years. She prayed long and hard for her wayward teenage daughter, often going into her child's room when she was not home and commanding the powers of darkness to leave her alone. She knew all the right words and used them frequently, but nothing happened.

The problem was her lack of understanding that warfare is accomplished on both the natural plane and the spiritual. The prayer warfare she practiced was legitimate, but she did not follow up in her actions. Her daughter cursed her, threatened her, and carried on a general attitude of contempt and disrespect. Evelyn did not correct the situation. She was afraid. She later admitted the fear that her daughter would be driven away if she exercised discipline.

Finally, in desperation, she sought wise counsel, and was advised that until she took her rightful authority in her own home, resisting the enemy on the girl's behalf would not accomplish anything. As Evelyn began to act on that advice, incorporating tough love principles of discipline into her home and prayer warfare life, her daughter responded. Although they aren't completely past the problem yet, much progress has been made.

Tough love (a concept we will discuss a little later) was not originated by a parent or group of parents who could not take it any longer; it is a principle of Scripture and it is a principle that severely hinders demonic activity. Parents must do battle in both the natural and spiritual realms. One arena of warfare must not be sacrificed at the expense of the other. Both the natural and spiritual realms must be examined, for placing too much emphasis on either is dangerous. Unfortunately, as we saw in Evelyn's case, most parents lack understanding in one or both areas.

Is it possible for demons to be involved in the attitudes of a son or daughter exhibiting bizarre, rebellious behavior? Without question, the answer is yes. Not only does Scripture teach that demons are real, but the experiences of far too many people are confirming this reality.

If you suspect that your child's behavior is demonically influenced, consider his or her behavior against the following list of characteristics:

- a radical change in personality;
- speech filled with hatred and bitterness;
- uncontrollable anger and rage;
- heavy amounts of blasphemy;

- radical change in moral values;
- interest in the occult;
- superhuman strength;
- voice change when the demon manifests;
- knowledge not learned through previous experiences;
- glassy eyes;
- listlessness and passivity;
- inability to control the desire for pornography, adultery, fornication, or homosexuality.

While not every person under the influence of a demon will act the same way, the above list indicates some things evident when a demon is present. At the same time, manifestation of some of these traits is not always indicative of demonic influence. If in doubt, seek counsel from those trained in discerning the presence of demon spirits, and ask God for discernment as well.

The Nature of Demons

Let's look closer at what demons actually are and what they do. Demons are spirit beings, apparently fallen angels who are set on destroying humanity (see Luke 22:31; 1 Peter 5:8; Eph. 6:10–12). The chaotic condition of our world is largely due to the influence of these unseen beings led by their master prince: "The whole world is under the control of the evil one" (1 John 5:19). His goal is to steal, kill, and destroy (see John 10:10).

Demons are not figments of our imagination. They are not concepts or ideas, nor do they run around dressed in red suits carrying pitchforks and sporting sharp tails. They are real beings. And although we do not see them with our natural eyes, they nevertheless possess characteristics much like our own—will, mind, and emotions.

Demons are not omnipresent; that is, unlike God, they can only be in one place at one time. They seek to destroy a person by waging war against his or her mind. Satan's basic tactic is to lie to the human mind. Jesus called him the "father of lies" (see John 8:44). Demons deceive people by teaching their own erroneous doctrines. "The Spirit clearly says that in later times some will abandon the faith and follow deceiving spirits and things taught by demons" (1 Tim. 4:1). Exactly how demons communicate to the human mind is not clear. What is clear is that the Scriptures teach they have this ability, and experience verifies it.

Think of it this way. A demon is like someone following you around all day, harassing you with subtle suggestions and yelling and shouting accusations. After a while you begin to believe the demon and respond to its input. A demon works to win a person over to his way of thinking, to wear him down with ongoing persuasion. Lacking the knowledge and power to ward off these spirit beings, a person will sooner or later yield to their influence.

Although we use the term "demon possession" to describe the deepest workings of a demon's spirit on the human's spirit (something that happens only in un-believers), the term is a kind of misnomer because in reality, a demon can possess or own nothing, since God owns everything (see Ps. 24:1; 50:9–12). In more recent times, Bible students have opted for a different term other than the word possession to describe the deeper workings of a demon. Instead of calling a person "demon possessed," many use the word *demonized,* meaning the influence of a demon in an unusually powerful way.

The first question a parent may ask concerning a child is, "Could my child be demonized?" The next question is, "Can a Christian be demonized?" Arguments for and against the idea range widely, for the subject holds some fear and disagreement.

We believe that Scripture teaches the answer is "yes" to both questions. A demon or demons can influence your child; in fact, demons can influence anyone, whether Christian or not. This is why we are warned in Scripture to put on the whole armor of God (see Eph. 6:10–20); to fight the good fight of faith (see 1 Tim. 6:12); and to be careful not to let the devil outwit us (see 2 Cor. 2:11).

The Influence of Demons

Note that, even in the presence of Jesus, Peter had problems with Satan. At one point the influence was so strong that Jesus turned and resisted Satan's work in Peter (see Matt. 16:21–23). Since demons can own nothing, their work is largely done through influence.

The more powerful the influence, the more bizarre the actions of the person involved.

Keep this in mind. The activity of demons upon Christians differs somewhat from the activity of demons upon unbelievers. In a Christian a demon cannot enter his spirit. That is the throne room where God takes up residence by his Holy Spirit once a person is converted. A demon can go only so far as the realm of a Christian's soul. There the battle rages for the mind. This is why we must put on the mind of Christ. In an unbeliever it is possible for a demon to influence and affect his spirit. Not only is his soul attacked, but his spirit as well. Look for a moment at the hideous attitudes displayed by the unregenerate (attitudes generated by the spirit) and it doesn't take long to see the influence of the enemy.

To understand how to resist and finally stop demon activity, remember that the mind is the battlefield. Actually, the enemy's plan is to captivate the entire soul area—will, mind, and emotions—so that access to the human spirit becomes possible. Again, remember a Christian has protection from being influenced in the spirit. "The one who is in you is greater than the one who is in the world" (1 John 4:4). The inner part of our being consists of two elements—soul and spirit (see Heb. 4:12). The enemy works on the soul life in order to get to the spirit. That is why it is so important to have Christ in this inner spirit sanctuary so that demon entrance is not possible.

And so the battle begins for the control of mankind.

The mind is assaulted, harassed, lied to, and struck at in every way so that it will give in to thoughts and ideas that lead to attitude changes. With the attitude changes comes a change of heart, and eventually the human spirit is in danger of falling captive to the enemy. (For further information on this subject, read *The Real Battle* by Ray Beeson; also, William Gurnall's book *The Christian in Complete Armor* is excellent.)

As long as the influence stays in the area of the soul, the battle will be one of oppression expressed by moods of discouragement and depression. Most rebellious teenagers would fit into this category. The Bible does not make a clear distinction between oppression and possession. This is why some people say Christians can be demon-possessed. What they mean is that Christians can be "demonized." Demonization of a Christian is influence in his soul, basically assaults upon his mind. In an unbeliever, it is possible for the influence to go further, that is, into his spirit.

Doing Battle Against Demons

When a Christian comes under powerful satanic attack—the attack of a demon—he or she may temporarily do some unusual things as a result. Generally our own spirit, with the help of the Holy Spirit, fights these mental attacks until they are pushed out and there is relief. Some attacks, however, become so overwhelming that the person needs help. In that case, intercessory prayer becomes necessary.

The following is an example of such intercessory

prayer. Note, however, before you begin that we must recognize our need for God's help in prayer (see Rom. 8:26):

> *Father, I come to You in the name of Jesus, on behalf of my son/daughter _____. I thank You, Lord, that You have given him/her to me as a heritage to love and raise to Your glory. I ask You to forgive me for my failures to lead and guide him/her in the way he/she ought to go. I thank You that You are the God who restores and who brings good out of evil.*
>
> *Take even my past failures, Lord, and use them to Your glory as You faithfully draw _____ to Yourself. I thank You that through You I am mighty and can pull down the strongholds of the enemy. I exercise that authority now in the mighty name of Jesus.*
>
> *And in Jesus' name I bind the powers of darkness that would blind _____ to Your truth and I command them to loose him/her now. And Father, in Jesus' name, I ask that You would draw _____ to Yourself, convicting him/her of sin by Your Holy Spirit. I plead the protection and deliverance of the blood of Jesus over _____ and by faith claim _____ for the Kingdom of God. In Jesus' name, Amen.*

Jesus clearly cast out demons by telling them verbally to leave. Before He left for heaven He deputized his followers to do the same (see John 14:12–13). He promised to give them power over demon spirits and over all the power of the enemy (see Luke 10:19).

Can you actually remove the influence of a demon from the life of an individual? We believe you can. Although doing so is not complicated, it is not as simple as it sounds and it is not magical. You do not recite a particular saying or prayer and see demons run for cover. They leave only because of Jesus. To try to exorcise or take authority over them apart from the name and power of Jesus Christ is not only futile, it is dangerous (see Acts 19:13–16). Jesus said that all power was given to Him, both in heaven and on earth (see Matt. 28:18). When Christians go to Christ and wait on Him, He bestows that power and the enemy's work is destroyed.

The process of deliverance involves many factors, all under the guidance of the Holy Spirit. First, the person affected by the demon must be willing to be set free. As long as an individual chooses to remain in rebellion, exorcism will not work. Even if the demon were exorcised, he would return to wreak more havoc than before (see Matt. 12:44–45; Luke 11:24–26). Second, when the rebellious person does not want deliverance, intercessory prayer becomes your most powerful weapon. Intercession is violent prayer. It not only storms heaven's gates looking for help, but turns that help into pushing demon spirits away from the rebellious person so that he or she can make proper choices. This takes time, sometimes months or even years. Prayer, then, becomes much more than the casual petition that so many believe it to be. Intercessory prayer is warfare (see Matt. 11:12 KJV). It is going to

God on behalf of someone else who needs deliverance from the presence of the enemy.

It may seem strange that intercessory prayer is a powerful weapon in the Christian's arsenal. We are far too used to the natural realm where brute force is our answer. But Paul declared:

> For though we live in the world, we do not wage war as the world does. The weapons we fight with are not the weapons of the world. On the contrary, they have divine power to demolish strongholds. We demolish arguments and every pretension that sets itself up against the knowledge of God, and we take captive every thought to make it obedient to Christ.
>
> (2 Cor. 10:3–5)

The reality of the demon realm may cause you to feel overwhelmed. Don't submit to those feelings. Thousands of people who now live overcoming lives had to walk the same road as you. Instead, learn step by step, moment by moment, the truths of God's Word necessary to bring you to victory. You may want to begin with this prayer:

Father God, the immensity of the war at hand seems overwhelming. I desire to have courage and make commitments that will lead to the defeat of the enemy in my life and the lives of others around me. I ask for Your help. I need wisdom, understanding, and discernment. Please strengthen me in spirit that I might fight the good fight of faith. Amen.

Chapter 7

Open Doors to Rebellion

❖ Looking back, Milt and Olivia can now identify the open door that provided entrance of the demonic influence that fostered their son's rebellion. Ross had been raised in church and had made a commitment to Jesus Christ as a young child, but at the age of ten he succumbed to temptation and peer pressure and smoked marijuana for the first time. Although his drug use was relatively light for the first few years, it slowly but surely drew him into a new lifestyle and a new mind-set—that of rebellion against authority. As the drug use escalated, so did his negative attitudes. By the time Olivia and Milt realized the magnitude of Ross's problem, rebellion had a firm foothold on his soul.

In order to create rebellion, demons try to gain access into a person's life through entry points we call doors. As natural enemies used to gain access to ancient cities through breaches in their walls, much the same is true for people. A demon has to have a point of entrance in order to influence and ultimately gain control. Knowing the entry points helps parents protect their children by heeding Paul's admonition in Ephesians 4:27, which warns against giving the devil a "foothold."

As the example of Milt and Olivia and their son Ross clearly demonstrates, the demon realm desires to destroy a person and those around him through the negative effects of rebellion. This is accomplished through attitudinal changes, or changes in the human spirit.

There are two things to consider in understanding what we mean by "spirit." The first is the deepest part of the person himself. The second is the attitude and influence a person (including demons) generates around him. We say, there is a certain "spirit" about a person.

It is easy to misunderstand how demon spirits work. For instance, someone may refer to a demonized person as having a demon spirit. We may then assume that the demon has somehow crawled into a person and is now under or inside his skin. Although this may be true in part, what is happening is that the spirit (attitudes) of that demon has affected the person. The more attitudes demons can affect, the more control they will exert.

People who walk together in close harmony are said to be one in spirit. This is most true, of course, within the one-flesh relationship of marriage. How many times have you met a husband and wife who have been together so long that they can finish each other's sentences? Marriage, however, is not the only relationship in which two people can become one in spirit. A student who is strongly influenced by a teacher, particularly over a long period of time, may become one in spirit with that teacher so that the student later teaches in much the same way as his or her mentor, even adopting some of the voice inflections and mannerisms of the teacher.

The closer two people become in spirit, the more they act alike. A demon or demons who walk in close harmony with a person will become one in spirit with that person. Since a demon, unlike a human being, is dispossessed of a natural body, its spirit is able to entangle itself around the human spirit and gain inner control.

Control of the human spirit is accomplished through control of the human mind, which of course is why the enemy works so hard on the thought life. It is also why the Bible teaches that we should think on good things (see Phil. 4:8) and why "we take captive every thought to make it obedient to Christ" (2 Cor. 10:5). The enemy of our soul seeks to control the mind, and he makes the mind his battlefield. Many people affirm they have difficulty controlling their thoughts. A ceaseless battle rages within, and the battle is not restricted to unbelievers.

What are some of the open doors through which the enemy attacks the mind? Consider anything that keeps a person from thinking clearly.

Drug Abuse

Illegal drugs are a definite door through which the enemy can gain access. For although a person may "feel good" while on drugs, proper function of his senses is greatly reduced. The mind becomes confused as to what signals to send so that everything functions properly. At this point the enemy can suggest actions that will not be appropriately examined and resisted. Young people are particularly susceptible to this, because their bodies are not yet fully matured and it takes a lesser amount of drugs to affect their physical and mental functions.

Ross's example of demonic influence making entrance through the open door provided by drug use is hardly a unique case. Illegal drug use has become so widespread that even the government acknowledges its inability to effectively curtail its use. This multi-billion dollar business is run in the natural world by ruthless drug lords, and controlled in the spirit realm by demonic hordes bent on the destruction of humanity. Even legal drugs can be dangerous, especially through misuse. If you believe they are necessary, make sure they are used according to prescription and only as your doctor advises.

Alcohol

Although not always regarded as such, alcohol is a drug, one which greatly reduces the mind's ability to respond adequately to foreign suggestions. Alcohol, even to minors, is easily accessible and has become the drug of choice among many young people today.

Alcohol is especially dangerous because its use is so prevalent and, within certain limits, even legally and socially acceptable. Christ-centered support groups designed for those seeking freedom from addictions have found that it is not unusual for longtime church members and respected citizens to join the group. They need help with problems stemming from alcohol use, much of which may have started as a "socially acceptable" method of dealing with the many stresses of everyday life.

Mind Control

Many cult leaders require unquestioned devotion to themselves. In a slow and very deceptive process, a person gives up his free will. The resulting passivity becomes fertile soil for the work of demon spirits. When a person ceases to use his mind and think for himself, other people, as well as demons, will try to make use of it. Because children are so impression-able, they are prime targets for these kinds of people.

This is why the Bible is clear on the necessity to "test the spirits to see whether they are from God, be-cause many false prophets have gone out into the world" (1 John 4:1). It even gives one method to recognize the Spirit of God as opposed to an evil spirit: "Every spirit that acknowledges that Jesus Christ has come in the flesh is from God, but every spirit that does not acknowledge Jesus is not from God. This is the spirit of the antichrist" (1 John 4:2–3).

A person who does not acknowledge (both in word and deed) "that Jesus Christ [representing both His humanity and His deity] has come in the flesh," is operating in a wisdom that "does not come down from heaven but is earthly, unspiritual, of the devil" (James 3:15).

Lack of Identity

One of the most prevalent open doors to demonic influence is a lack of identity, or sense of worth. A child who lacks a secure environment, a loving family and a sense of acceptance within that family, will fail to assimilate an identity of his or her own. Instead, that child will seek to identify with the world around him. He will attach bits and pieces of identity from others, becoming a "chameleon" of sorts, and blend in with his or her surroundings in an attempt to be accepted. This sort of child is wide open to any negative peer pressure that comes along, as well as subtle demon influence.

Environment

We are also influenced through our senses. That is why the advertisement industry makes great use of sight and sound. Advertisers know that the correct influence of these two senses will result in the desire for and eventual purchase of their products.

Similarly, the world, as well as demon spirits, uses the senses to sell its products. "The Spirit clearly says that in later times some will abandon the faith and follow deceiving spirits and things taught by demons" (1 Tim. 4:1). To rationalize that nightclubs will not hurt you or that certain types of music will do no harm is to court disaster. The influence always works to affect the mind in ways that allow negative attitudes and ruinous actions.

The Occult

Spiritualistic "toys" such as Ouija boards, crystal balls, and tarot cards, along with palm reading and horoscopes, provide one of the greatest avenues for influence from demon spirits. Trances, mediumistic or clairvoyant powers, and magical abilities are all the work of demons. Crystals, charms, amulets, talismans, good-luck pieces, fetishes, and any other such items thought to possess power provide entrance points for demons to work (see Deut. 18:10, 11; 2 Kings 23:24).

Christian author Maria Metlova Kearns knows this truth all too well. As a young Russian woman trying to make a living in the United States, she got involved in fortune-telling as a gimmick, thinking it a harmless joke to play on gullible people. Before she became too deeply entrenched in this demonic activity, however, she agreed to "pass on" her talent to a close friend.

Years later, after Maria had become a Christian and re-nounced her former occultic involvement, she real-ized how very real and dangerous her fortune-telling had been. She is still praying for deliverance for her former friend who inherited Maria's fortune-telling talent—Jean Dixon.

Many people enter the realm of demons thinking they are simply traveling another avenue toward God. The Bible, however, makes it extremely clear that there is only one way to get to God, and that is through His Son, Jesus Christ (see John 14:6); all other ways lead to death and destruction (see Prov. 14:12).

The Bible also makes it clear that occultic activity does not come from God. Occultic activity slips in de-ceptively. Palm readers, psychics, and channelers ap-pear to many to be avenues through which God can work. On the contrary, God warns us against them. These people have been deceived by demons.

> Do not turn to mediums or seek out spiritists, for you
> will be defiled by them. I am the LORD your God.
>
> (Lev. 19:31)

> I will set my face against the person who turns to
> mediums and spiritists to prostitute himself by follow-
> ing them, and I will cut him off from his people.
>
> (Lev. 20:6)

> A man or woman who is a medium or spiritist among
> you must be put to death. You are to stone them; their
> blood will be on their own heads.
>
> (Lev. 20:27)

For such men are false apostles, deceitful workmen, masquerading as apostles of Christ. And no wonder, for Satan himself masquerades as an angel of light. It is not surprising, then, if his servants masquerade as servants of righteousness. Their end will be what their actions deserve.

(2 Cor. 11:13–15)

In addition, note the following Scriptures:

Witchcraft, sorcery, and wizardry (communicating with demon spirits): Ex. 22:18; 1 Sam. 15:23; 28:3, 9; 2 Kings 9:22; 21:6; 2 Chron. 33:6; Isa. 47:9, 12; 57:3; Jer. 27:9; Dan. 2:2; Mic. 5:12; Nah. 3:4; Mal. 3:5; Acts 8:9–11; 13:6–8; Gal. 5:19–21; Rev. 18:23; 21:8; 22:15.
Soothsaying and divination (fortune-telling): Num. 22:7; 23:23; Deut. 18:10–14; 2 Kings 17:17; 1 Sam. 6:2; Isa. 2:6; Jer. 14:14; 27:9; 29:8; Ez. 12:24; 13:6–7; 21:22–29; 22:28; Dan. 2:27; 4:7; 5:7, 11; Mic. 3:7; 5:12; Zech. 10:2; Acts 16:16.

Not only are each of the areas mentioned above open doors for demonic activity, it is not unusual for participation in one area to lead to participation in another. To dabble in any of these is to invite demonic influence and activity within our lives.

What this means to parents is that, not only must we be pure in excluding these things from our own lives, we must do everything possible, both practically and spiritually, to see that our children stay free of them as well. Vigilance in prayer, family devotions, quality time with our children, and monitoring the type of education and peer pressure they are exposed to are just some of the ways to help guard against these open doors in our children's lives.

Heredity

The power of generational sin is strong, and yet it is seldom understood. Demon influence is sometimes handed down from family to family. The effects of a demon on a parent, sometimes displayed in attitudes can be picked up by their children. Scripture speaks of punishment for the sin of idol worship being carried out to the third and fourth generation (see Deut. 5:8–9).

Society is catching up in its understanding of what the Bible has taught along these lines for thousands of years, although modern thinking may not acknowledge the word "sin" in this hereditary factor. It is now understood that abusing parents were usually abused as children; children with addictive problems such as alcohol or drugs frequently have at least one parent with a similar problem; and the list goes on. Our influence over our children extends far beyond those things we see in the natural realm.

Satanic influence from family to succeeding family is powerful. We are often unaware of how powerful the influence is largely because we are unaware of the enemy's devices. If we understood the power of influence and what it does, we would be careful both in what we allow to be passed *to* us and what we allow to be passed *through* us. In examining Satan's doctrines—and he does teach doctrines (see 1 Tim. 4:1)—you'll find that all of them are not of a theological nature. Satan's hosts of evil spirits also inspire pessimistic thoughts such as, "I'm no good"; "I'm a failure"; "My kids will never amount to anything"; "I deserve better than this." These thoughts are picked up and passed on to the next generation.

God wants generational sin to stop. Although not discounting the validity of the term "dysfunctional families," much of the dysfunction perpetuated through the generations is nothing less than generational sin. Victims become victors by determining to allow God to intervene and cut off the sin. God is not less compassionate than we are. He wants us delivered. But He has a procedure for doing so that incorporates a relationship with Jesus and a cleansing that comes only through His blood.

The first step to break the hold of generational sin is to accept Jesus Christ as your own personal Savior. If you have done that, then the next step is to ask the Holy Spirit to search your heart and reveal to you any unconfessed sins (see 1 Chron. 28:9; Ps. 139:23–24) so that you may confess them and be forgiven and cleansed and restored to righteousness (see 1 John 1:9). Then, pray aloud the following prayer of confession for the sins of your ancestors (either verbatim or use it as a model):

Father God, in the mighty name of Jesus Christ, I come to You now to repent on behalf of my family line. Lord, wherever there was the sin of _____ on my father's or on my mother's side, I repent of that sin on behalf of my family, both on the (father's family name) *side and on the* (mother's family name) *side.*

Wherever I had an ancestor who yielded to this particular sin, even as far back as Adam, I ask You to forgive us as a family and to cleanse the family line of this sin by the blood of Jesus. Wherever You see an invisible soul-tie that connects me with any of those people who yielded to this sin, I now take a sword in the spirit and in the name of Jesus Christ I sever that connection in the spirit and I break every unholy soul-tie between myself and those previous generations.

And I now place a river of the blood of Jesus between myself and those generations and render myself free from any unholy influence. I also break any curse that has come to me or my children through generational sin. In Jesus' name and according to Deuteronomy 23:5, I ask You to turn the curses into blessings. Amen.

Pray this prayer as many times as necessary, each time you identify a generational sin operating within your family. This prayer works to break the curse of generational sin at your generation. However, if you already have children, you will need to understand that, although the curse can no longer torment you or be passed through you to future children you might have when it is broken, the generational sin may already be at work in your existing children.

We must continue in active and violent intercession for those children, daily committing them to God, remembering that God has promised, "I will contend with those who contend with you, and your children I will save" (Isa. 49:25). We must continue to fight the enemy in the name of Jesus, in the power of His Spirit, following in His steps, and entrusting our children to Him if ever they are to come to a saving knowledge of Jesus Christ and be rescued from the clutches of darkness.

When we have done that, we will have helped them close the doors to demonic influence and future rebellion.

Chapter 8

Lasting Impressions

❖ Carl wasn't more than about five years old when he caught a trout in the stream running through his grandfather's farm. He was so excited about his catch that he ran to show the still wiggling fish to his grandfather, who soundly corrected him for not killing it first.

Rick enjoyed shop classes at school and did very well with machine work. After completing a project, he took it home to show his parents. Rick remembers his dad sitting for a very long time, scrutinizing every detail of the work, looking to find something wrong. His father couldn't stop until he discovered an extremely small, almost undetectable flaw.

Both Carl and Rick speak of their experiences with bitterness. Carl's experience was more than thirty-five years ago, Rick's more than twenty-five; yet, to each of these men, it seems like yesterday. Neither can leave it alone.

Dr. Kevin Leman and Randy Carlson, authors of *Unlocking the Secrets of Your Childhood Memories,* begin their book with a promise: "Tell us about your earliest childhood memories, and we'll tell you about yourself today."[1] These two Christian psychologists are convinced that early childhood memories—and that definitely includes the words spoken to us by those most significant people in our lives, i.e., our parents—make lasting impressions that carry over into every aspect of our adult lives.

Words That Destroy

Scolding and critical statements leave devastating marks on people. They actually make up the second of two steps that will send our children in the wrong direction, silence being the first step. Even if the negative statements are left out, people—especially young people—still need praise and encouragement for emotional stability and to enhance personal performance. As one youth pastor put it, "Young people are not looking for people to point the finger *at* them, but rather for people to point the way *for* them."

We live in a performance oriented society. Since Sputnik was launched into space in 1957 by the Soviets, there has been a greater emphasis on education, with an underscore on success. We are so caught up in the success syndrome that we have become an extremely self-conscious society. This gives us just that much more of a need for approval and support.

Words are powerful tools for affecting behavior:

> Likewise the tongue is a small part of the body, but it makes great boasts. Consider what a great forest is set on fire by a small spark. The tongue also is a fire, a world of evil among the parts of the body. It corrupts the whole person, sets the whole course of his life on fire, and is itself set on fire by hell.
>
> (James 3:5–6)

Gary Smalley and John Trent, in their book _The Blessing,_ tell what a single word did to a young boy:

> Let us tell the story of Mean Mike. Actually, this young man's name is only Mike, but his family began calling him this when he was a toddler. Why "Mean Mike"? Mike had a terrific grip as a young child; and if anyone tried to take something away from him, he would snarl and hold on for dear life. Their nickname of Mean Mike began as a humorous way to picture this bulldog tenacity in holding onto something. But the nickname soon became much more than that; it became the way he lived his life.
>
> Today "Mean Mike" is in state prison in Arizona. Isn't it sad how children can live up to their negative nicknames? Mike certainly did, and it set a tragic course for his life.[2]

The story of Mean Mike illustrates an important lesson: by tagging someone, particularly an impressionable child, with a nickname, that child may very well reinforce the behavior signified by that name. When the name is negative, we have set in motion what could easily become a negative lifestyle, one with tragic results.

The words we speak to our children, including the nicknames we tag them with, can also be used for or against our children in the spiritual realm. The Old Testament is full of examples of how people were blessed or cursed by words spoken to them or over them. In fact, the family blessing, usually spoken by the father and reserved for the firstborn, was a much coveted honor (see Gen. 27).

As much as we love our children, we often do not think about the words we speak to them or the names we brand them with. We bless or curse our children with our words, which is why we must choose our words carefully and bestow blessings upon them, rather than curses. For instance, rather than verbally labeling a child as "hopeless" because of the negative things we see in his or her life, we can, instead, speak to the child of the future. For example, "In spite of the problems you are dealing with right now, I am thankful that God has given you to us to love and to raise to His glory. I know that He is going to do great things in your life." Although your child may not show any positive reaction to such statements of blessing, a blessing has been bestowed rather than a curse; eventually the benefits will be reaped. This is called walking "by faith, not by sight" (2 Cor. 5:7), and calling "things that are not as though they were" (Rom. 4:17).

Attitudes That Communicate

Attitudes of disrespect are sometimes carried out in other ways besides words. For instance, what is a parent who flies off the handle, either in word or in deed, communicating to a child? First, the parent may very well be reacting inappropriately due to his or her own mood, thus causing confusion for the child who is unable to relate the parent's reaction to the situation. Second, this sort of parental reaction communicates that the parent-child relationship is based on the young person's ability to perform. If the child does everything perfectly as expected, he or she will not get punished. It says nothing about one of the most fundamental needs of our existence—the need to be loved aside from our performance, aside from our abilities or lack of them. We need to be loved unconditionally, no strings attached—loved just because we are, because we exist.

In addition to intercessory prayer, discussed in chapter 7 and again in chapter 13, another powerful weapon at our disposal in the fight to rescue our children from the enemy is our love. Nothing is more terrifying to the enemy of our soul than a love that just will not quit. This love says, both in words and actions, that although I may not approve of or support what you do, I will still love you. The Father used that kind of love to defeat the devil at Calvary—and that kind of love can be found nowhere except through a personal relationship with the One who went to Calvary.

In other words, even while our children are in the midst of rebellion, our love toward them should never change. And our children must be clearly aware of this fact. We must convey love to them constantly. Following are some suggestions for expressing this love to your children verbally:

- Honey, although we cannot condone your behavior and must deal with you according to that behavior, that does not change the fact that we love you.
- I know you think that love is letting you do what you think you want to do, but that is very far from love.
- Your behavior has become increasingly destructive, both to yourself and to the rest of the family. We have to do everything possible to stop that destructive behavior, but we want you to understand that we have not stopped loving you. We love you just as much as we did before you became involved in this type of behavior, and just as much as we will when you stop behaving in such a destructive manner.
- Although your behavior requires us to deal differently with you than with your brothers and sisters

who are not behaving in a destructive manner, we want you to know that we love you all equally.

If we are careful to express and to model that kind of love toward them, we will do extensive damage to the work of the enemy upon their lives. We will also be more likely to deal with their rebellious behavior in a way that brings healing and restoration, rather than revenge and retribution. The frequent, honest, sincere use of the three little words, "I love you," *even if the rebellious child does not respond,* can be a good starting place when other words seem to fail us. And the lasting impression that is made by those words is not one the child will easily forget.

Jesus did not come to earth to reconcile us to the Father by condemning us (see John 3:17). He did it by extending God's love to us. Condemnation and fault-finding do nothing to restore our wayward teenagers to the family. Remember, "God's kindness leads you toward repentance" (Rom. 2:4).

The father of the prodigal son knew that. And that's the kind of love he modeled toward his son—a love that left an indelible impression on the boy, even after he had chosen to leave the safety and security of his family home. When the son finally "came to his senses" and decided to return home, his father welcomed him with open arms (see Luke 15:11–32), leaving a lasting impression not only on his son but on the millions of readers who have been so impacted by this story through the years.

Experiences That Condemn

Walking in God's all-forgiving love is the most powerful kind of spiritual warfare we can wage, and the most positive, lasting impression we can ever impart to our children. At the same time, we need to be careful to clarify the difference between love and approval. Love—all-forgiving, unconditional love—focuses on who we are. Approval focuses on what we do.

Sometimes what is considered to be an expression of love is really an expression of approval. We congratulate our children for a good report card. We thank them for doing a good job of mowing the lawn or washing the dishes. We comment on how well-dressed they are. And for every statement we make in this regard, we say they have our attention because they are doing well.

But they need something for the in-between times as well. They need positive affirmation when they aren't doing anything at all. And they especially need our unconditional love when they are experiencing failure or rejection, or even the self-induced results of rebellion. Only unconditional love will build character in them that isn't based on performance. Regardless of their actions or inactions, they *are* something and they *are* someone simply because they exist. And few things in life seem more valuable than that.

Dr. James Dobson, well known Christian psychologist and author, discusses this warped sense of values on which we base our love and estimation of our children's worth in his best-selling book *Hide or Seek:* "Without question, the most highly valued personal attribute in our culture (and in most others) is physical attractiveness." He goes on to say, "If beauty represents the primary ingredient of self-esteem and worthiness, the second most important attribute in our culture is certainly intelligence."[3]

A child who does not excel in a particular area, and who may not be extremely good looking or intelligent, could grow up with a low self-esteem level if his parents haven't consistently reinforced their unconditional love for him through words and actions. And even those children who might be success-oriented or good looking or intelligent could still have a wrong opinion of themselves if they grow up thinking that their parents' love for them is based on those particular attributes. All have value simply because they are precious gifts to their parents from a loving God.

Our society certainly does not help us instill the concept of unconditional love in our children. How many times have you heard a news report about a young person being killed in some sort of accident, and the reporter adds some inane remark along the lines of, "What makes this loss so tragic is the fact that this young man was so well liked, did well in school, and played first string on the high school football team." Does that imply that, had the same young man not been well liked, done well in school, and played first string on the football team, the degree of tragedy would be less? No wonder despondent teens with little or no self-esteem are taking their own lives at an alarming rate! They've been programmed to believe that their lives aren't all that important anyway, so what have they or their family or society got to lose?

Another danger is to confuse love with a different kind of approval, the sanctioning of a lifestyle. God hates sin but He loves the sinner. Gordon Aeschliman, in his book *Cages of Pain,* tells the story of a bruised and tired prostitute who sought God:

> Michelle had no self-worth left. She was the soiled rag of men's pleasures, and she had even failed in taking her own life. She came to God's sanctuary pleading and broken. You learn as a prostitute to grovel in the presence of authority, and so she did in the presence of God, vulnerable as a disobedient dog that cowers in wait for the master's sentence. Will it be mercy or will it be punishment?
>
> For Michelle it was punishment: Halfway through the church service the pastor recognized her. Before the entire congregation, he lectured Michelle for defiling the house of God with her filthy presence and ordered her out.[4]

How tragic that a man who was supposed to represent a loving and forgiving God instead chose to chastise and condemn. Unlike the woman caught in adultery and brought before Jesus for judgment, only to receive forgiveness and a chance for a new life (see

John 8:3–11), this woman went away unforgiven, more sure than ever of her unworthiness and hopeless condition.

As parents, situations often require us to love our children unconditionally, in spite of the fact that we can in no way condone their destructive behavior. We must make this clear to them when we confront them with the error of their chosen lifestyle, reassuring them that, although we may be forced to take drastic measures as a result of that lifestyle, we will never, ever stop loving them.

Lives That Model

It starts when they're little. That undeserved, unchanging, unending love that God has so graciously bestowed on us must be modeled to our children from the moment we receive them into this world—in both our actions and in the words we speak. If, however, you are reading this book and thinking, I was not aware of that sort of love when my children were little, nor did I know how to model it, don't be discouraged.

The Bible is full of promises about restoration. The important thing is to start where you are. If your child is already a rebellious teenager, it is not too late to apologize for not having shown that sort of love in the past. You can assure your child that, even while not approving or condoning the present rebellious behavior, you will make every effort by the grace of God to show that love in the future. As your children begin to experience and grow in the knowledge of that love, regardless of their age, they will more readily comprehend and receive that same love from their heavenly Father.

Positive lasting impressions on our children come only as we learn to speak the truth in love (see Eph. 4:15). Admittedly, this isn't always easy, even under the best of circumstances. When you are dealing with someone who exhibits very little love and has long-since lost touch with the truth, it is especially difficult. At times, we may feel like giving up. After all, effective communication is a two-way street, and if the conversation from one of the parties involved has degenerated into monosyllabic grunts, why bother?

Why bother? Because God tells us to, that's why. "Speaking the truth in love" is not a suggestion; it is an imperative if ever we are to "grow up into him who is the Head, that is, Christ" (Eph. 4:15). Speaking the truth in love, therefore, implies maturation, a "growing up" process, one that needs to be modeled to our offspring just as we must model to them the other aspects of growing into maturity. If we can't (or won't) make an effort to walk in God's truth and love, how can we expect our children to learn it?

In addition to speaking the truth in love to our children, both in word and in deed, another crucial aspect to leaving positive lasting impressions on them is listening. You cannot speak the truth in love if you have not first learned the art of listening. If your mind is preoccupied with what you are going to say as soon as the other person quits talking, you are not listening. Your child will be left with a lasting impression that is anything but positive.

Although disagreements over finances, children, and careers cause tremendous friction in marriage, the majority of family counselors agree that the primary source of marital discord is lack of effective communication. Counselors' offices are bursting at the seams with people needing to learn communication skills and the communication skill we most need to cultivate is listening. True, counselors do more than listen, but listening is a huge part of their job. A good counselor will always spend much more time listening than speaking. The same must be said for parents who desire to cultivate and maintain open and effective communication with their children.

Your children will be much more apt to approach you with their problems if they know they will be met with listening ears, rather than condemning words. This does not mean that you cannot respond to them once they have had a chance to fully voice their concerns, but the fact that you take the time to listen before speaking accomplishes two things: it reassures your child that you care and will respond in truth and love, and it better enables you to do just that.

Proverbs 18:13 warns, "He who answers before listening—that is his folly and his shame." If you only half listen to what your child is telling you, you may very well jump to conclusions and give a faulty answer based on a poor knowledge of the truth of the situation. In addition, even if you do understand the situation correctly, answering hastily will keep you from answering in love, since haste is usually fueled by anger or fear.

A great hindrance to family communication is the television and newspaper. We sometimes come home tired, wanting to relax, and therefore turn to one of these two distractions from our busy day. About the same time, a child or spouse wants our attention for a moment. What we do next tells our families what is most important in our lives. To lay the paper down or turn off the television can lead to some of the most meaningful moments in our lives. We communicate to our families, You are more important than newspaper, television, or even my need for a few moment's rest.

However, what if, even after taking the time to give our families our undivided attention and trying to cultivate good family communication skills, we find we still have a problem? For instance, after patiently listening to our child explain a situation, suppose we realize that we do not have enough truth or love within ourselves at that moment to wisely respond to his or her words?

At that point, the best thing a parent can do is say, "I'm not real clear on how to handle this right now. Until I've had time to think it through and to pray [and to discuss it with your spouse, if you have one] let's just put it on hold until [pinpoint a specific, reasonable time]." Even a rebellious child will appreciate the honesty of that response over a reactionary explosion. It may also help curb a child's tendency to lie to avoid inappropriate parental responses.

As much as we might like to deny it, the burden of effective communication within our families lies with us, not with our children. Parents who are seeking to communicate with each other and with their children must speak the truth in love. Remember that speaking the truth in love is a maturation process, one which must be modeled by the already mature to those who are beginning to mature. We cannot expect our children to share their problems and concerns with us if we have not made ourselves accessible to them. If every time they approach us we are either too busy or too cranky to take the time to really listen, then we are not leaving them with positive lasting impressions, and they will simply stop approaching us.

In order to leave positive lasting impressions on our children, we must learn to listen with our hearts, measure our words, focus on the truth, and sprinkle liberally everything we say with love, love, and more love. Regardless of the reaction—or lack thereof—that we may see in our teenagers, that truth and that love will impact them more deeply than we can imagine. And someday, when they too have learned to model lives that leave positive lasting impressions on others, they will communicate their gratitude to us—not only in words, but in the way they choose to rear their own children.

Chapter 9

Where Do We Turn?

❖ When Julie experienced problems with her fifteen-year-old son, Brad, her friends advised her to inform him that he could either "shape up or ship out." The friends, Bob and Suzie, had done that with their formerly rebellious daughter, Liz, and Liz had been so frightened at the prospect of facing life on the streets that she had "shaped up" immediately. When Julie took her friends' advice and offered the same ultimatum to Brad, he took her at her word and left home. She hasn't heard from him in two years.

Marian, on the other hand, assumes that everything is a spiritual problem and should only be handled by spiritual means. When her sister, Lois, confided in her that she suspected her fourteen-year-old daughter was involved with drugs, Marian advised her to "bind the powers of darkness and cast them out of her house and out of her daughter's life" once and for all. According to Marian, that would take care of the problem. When it didn't, Lois began to question her faith.

What well-meaning Bob and Suzie, as well as Marian, didn't realize was that their friends' problems with their children were both spiritual and physical, and needed to be handled accordingly. Bob and Suzie saw the problem as physical and offered simplistic advice from a physical standpoint, just as Marian did from the spiritual standpoint. Rebellion begins in the spiritual realm and is acted out in the physical realm; therefore, it must be dealt with in both areas. And it should not be done without first seeking God, as well as sound counsel and advice. A one-time "quick fix" is not the answer for these problems. Patient, loving concern that is committed for the long haul is.

We parents are usually shocked when we discover that our children are involved in illegal or immoral behavior. We immediately race off to solve the problem, only to become disillusioned when we discover that we cannot "fix" our children's lives overnight. And, if we are willing to admit it, most of us do not know what to do when a teenager initially goes astray. All the good advice we may have wanted to give other parents when they were having trouble suddenly seems trivial and worthless.

Parents who persist in dealing with the problem by themselves violate both sound judgment and the Scriptures (see Prov. 11:14; Gal. 6:2; James. 5:16). No parent is aware of all that is happening in our culture and thus able to speak to the many problems his or her children face. We need instruction and understanding ourselves in order to help. Scripture tells us to share our burdens with one another.

Turn to the Lord

But before we turn anywhere, we must first turn to God. Christ is our only source of help against the enemy of our soul and against his insidious attacks upon our children. Too many teenagers have been influenced by demons, and all the counsel in the world will not remove these evil beings from their encroachment. Nothing but the authority found in Christ will solve the problems of a teenager or anyone else who is deeply affected by the powers of hell.

Our first step as parents, then, is to make sure we are personally in league with the One who has all power both in heaven and on earth. From here we must train spiritually by putting on the whole armor of God (see Eph. 6:10–20). This, in turn, better prepares us to do warfare on behalf of our children.

But spiritual warfare is not the only way our problems are solved. Doing spiritual warfare cannot be substituted for education and discipline. By the same token, education and discipline cannot be substituted for doing spiritual warfare. Each has its place. The natural and spiritual realms go together to form a powerful bond.

Turning to Christ may not be easy for some people,

and the restoration of our children must not be the only reason we reach out to God. We must be fully convinced of our own personal need of Him or the relationship will have no power. At the same time, the Bible promises that if we come to Him with an open heart, He will not turn us away but will receive us as His own (see John 6:37), and will come into our lives, even as we invite Him to do so (see Rev. 3:20).

Romans 10:9–10 explains the simplicity of receiving Jesus as Lord and Savior:

> That if you confess with your mouth, "Jesus is Lord," and believe in your heart that God raised him from the dead, you will be saved. For it is with your heart that you believe and are justified, and it is with your mouth that you confess and are saved.

Fellowship with Others

In reaching out to God, the scriptural mandate is that we fellowship with other believers. We need people who will pray for us, give us encouragement, and direct us to solutions for the problems we face. Often we are encouraged simply by realizing that we are not alone. Many other parents have had to work through the devastating experiences surrounding a child who persists in destructive behavior. Many of these same people can now be excellent sources of advice and encouragement.

Finding a place of Christian fellowship may not be easy. Although there are churches almost every place you go, a church of understanding and compassion often has to be sought out. In some churches you may find the compassion, but not an understanding of how to deal with rebellion in both the natural and spiritual realms.

If your own church cannot deal with the problem, look for an auxiliary group. Although not a Christian organization, Tough Love provides some real insights into how to deal with kids who have gone astray, and the group has chapters across the nation. However, because this group does not approach the problem of teenage rebellion from a totally biblical angle, we advise parents to find a Christian support group that does understand and practice the biblical as well as the practical principles for dealing with this problem.[1]

Know the Laws

Once you are supported with spiritual, emotional, and practical help, you need to understand the local and state laws which protect parents and children. Contrary to some opinions, the government does not lie in wait to steal your child from you at the first opportunity. Although the government does not operate on biblical principles, it can still be our ally when it comes to dealing with an out-of-control teenager.

Some parents have been intimidated by their own children to the point of withholding deserved and needed discipline for fear that the child will report them to a child protective agency. Our answer to that is, do what you need to do, and inform your child that, should he or she choose to report you, the agency may very well step in and remove that child from the home.

However, also inform the child that he or she may then find that the alternative living arrangements are much less pleasant than what he or she had at home. For instance, the rules that so upset the child at home may also be reinforced in his new situation, along with additional rules. And where these rules were carried out with love at home, they may now be carried out with cool detachment, and with very little room for grace or compromise. Making sure your child is aware of this and refusing to be blackmailed may cause him or her to think twice before issuing threats.

In severe cases, when even minor skirmishes with the law have occurred and parents have tried every-thing to remedy the situation—restrictions, loss of privileges, counseling, etc.—and the child still refuses to accept parental authority, he or she may sometimes be turned over to the court system at the parents' re-quest. The key here is that the child must already have entered the legal system at some point, whether it be through repeated attempts at running away or arrests for illegal behavior. If the child has not yet become in-volved in the system, the state usually will not accept responsibility for assuming custody.

Many parents, especially single parents, need au-thoritative help. Some Christian parents may struggle with turning to a worldly governmental system, but the laws of the land exist for the benefit of Christians as much as anyone else.

Fourteen-year-old Jenny's parents became alarmed at the sudden change in their daughter's behavior. Formerly a sweet, compliant child, Jenny began to break curfew, talk back to her parents, lose interest in school and other activities, and spend time exclusively with a boy she'd recently met. An increasingly passionate romance with Jeff soon led to trouble when he insisted on seeing her regardless of the wishes of her parents. Jenny was pulled between the still smoldering embers of a desire to obey her parents and the emotional pressure exerted by Jeff. It finally took a court restraining order to solve the problem. For a small fee, Jenny's parents contacted an attorney and together they worked things out. If Jenny and Jeff wish to see each other, it must now be on Jenny's parents' terms. (More detailed information on the possible legalities involved when dealing with a rebellious teen can be found in a later chapter.)

Suppose you've just been informed that your son has been arrested for possession of marijuana. Or you've just found out that your daughter is pregnant. Or you've found a note telling you that your sixteen year old has run away. What do you do?

Have a Strategy

First, take some time to sort through your emotions. Anger, fear, worry, and blame are but a few elements of the trauma you may feel. This is normal. But if your child is to be rescued, you will need to recognize your responsibility to help lead this young person toward restoration.

Next, form a plan. Get informed. Gather all the information you can. Find out what your child has done and is still doing. Parent support groups can be a great help in giving you direction in how to go about this. When possible, find out the reasons for your child's actions. Check to see if there are any legal implications. For instance, if your son is over eighteen (sixteen in some states) and has gotten a minor pregnant, he may face a statutory rape charge. Depending on the circumstances and on the court, he could be in serious trouble. Also, contact school officials to get their input in solving the problem. Request that each of your child's teachers call you for a short telephone conference. Most teachers care about their students and are more than willing to cooperate in any way possible.

When seeking ways to help your child solve his or her problem, consider the most effective disciplinary actions, always keeping in mind that discipline should be viewed mostly as correction and not as punishment. Punishment comes from a principle of retribution. And, if there are legal implications for your child's problems, enough punishment and retribution will be incurred by the state; he or she does not need more of the same from you.

Larry had never been in trouble as an adolescent until he turned seventeen. That's when his father deserted the family, and Larry was devastated. In a knee-jerk reaction, he went out and got drunk, then got into a fight, seriously injuring someone. When it came time for his sentencing, his mother was asked by the probation department what she thought the sentence should be for her son.

As difficult as it was, Larry's mother gave the only answer she felt she could as a loving Christian parent. "I have prayed about it," she explained to the probation officer who, although not a Christian, reacted positively to this mother's obvious concern for her son's welfare. "And I have asked the Lord to do whatever He knows best, whatever is necessary to restore my son to the place he was before he got into trouble. I know my son's crime was caused, in part, by his father's desertion; however, I feel that Larry made a conscious choice to do what he did, even though he knew it was wrong. Therefore, I will accept whatever sentence he receives as the just punishment for his crime, but I will also stand by him through the whole thing, no matter what happens." Due to extenuating circumstances, Larry received a relatively light sentence of thirty days in a juvenile facility. His mother did not extend the punishment in any way when he was released; she felt he had paid for his crime, and she wanted him to know she was there to love him unconditionally and to help him move toward complete restoration. A wise mother indeed!

Eliminate Other Problems

Keep a few other points in mind when deciding how to deal with your child's rebellion. First, are you sure there are no physical reasons contributing to the problem? Second, are you and your spouse in agreement as to how to deal with the problem? And, third, are you sure you are not exaggerating the problem due to an unwillingness to allow your child to grow up?

Concerning the physical aspects, eliminate any medical reasons for your child's problems before deciding how to deal with the rebellion. Have you checked for attention deficit disorder or other physiologically induced behavioral problems? Medical reasons must first be evaluated before deciding on any course of action in dealing with your child's destructive behavior.

The second point—agreeing with your spouse on how to deal with your child's rebellion—is probably one of the biggest hurdles you will face. Often, one parent either downplays or overreacts to the problem. At the same time, the other parent, wanting to compensate for his or her spouse's inappropriate reactions, goes perhaps too far in the other direction. Hence, the problem remains unsolved.

Disagreement over how to raise children is a common cause of marital friction as counselors can attest. Because we tend to parent as we were parented and because no two people come from the same exact family-of-origin situation, it follows that no two people will agree on every single aspect of how to parent. Many children notice this difference of opinion between their parents early and play one against the other moving the focus off the child's behavior and onto the parents' disagreement.

Parents of a problem teenager should recognize this and get help immediately. The most obvious place for help is to go to the Lord together in prayer. In addition, pastors and Christian counselors can guide you through disciplinary decisions during this crisis time. Parent support group leaders can also help to effect a meeting of the minds in this area. A united front is vital if you are going to help your child move from rebellion to wholeness.

Third, are you misinterpreting your child's normal "spreading of the wings"—that necessary and progressive moving from total dependence on Mom and Dad to maturity and independence—as rebellion? We discussed this difference in detail in chapter 1. Although it is a difference that can be misunderstood by any parent, it most often happens with overprotective parents who just cannot stand to cut that umbilical cord. And yet, it must be cut, if ever our children are going to lead normal, healthy lives.

If you're not sure whether your child's behavior is normal or rebellious, examine his or her attitudes. Is he or she making these moves toward independence in a respectful manner? Is he or she making every effort to do so within the guidelines you have set? At the same time, how is your attitude? Are your guidelines realistic and in line with biblical truth? Are they being administered in love? Again, if you are unsure, a Christian parent support group can help you make this distinction.

Trust God

One final note: recognize that most people will be anxious to give advice. Some of it may be valid, some of it may not. You must sift through the information and discard what doesn't work for you or is just plain not biblical. This applies to both practical and spiritual advice, as Pam's situation so vividly exemplifies.

Pam was careful to raise her two children according to biblical guidelines, disciplining them firmly while at the same time surrounding them with an atmosphere of unconditional love and acceptance. Still, when her oldest child, Steven, turned thirteen, he began to run around with a new peer group, listening to music with lyrics that glorified drugs, sex, and violence.

As Pam steadfastly refused to allow this type of music to be played in her home, Steven grew more and more defiant and rebellious. At fourteen, he ran away. The police brought him back several times, but finally were unable to locate him. For an entire year, Pam had no idea where he was, or even if he was dead or alive. Loving friends and family supported her in prayer and offered advice as she waited out the long days and even longer nights. But in the long run, she had to sift through all that advice and seek God's direction each step of the way. When Steven was finally found, the judge decided the boy would simply run away again if returned home, so he was placed in a foster home.

Just as Pam finally accepted the temporary loss of her son, Steven's sister, Maggie, followed in her brother's footsteps. She ran away just before her sixteenth birthday and stayed gone over a year, living with an older woman she met on the streets. Just a couple of weeks before Christmas, however, Maggie called her mother and told her she wanted to come home.

"It's been an incredible readjustment period," Pam explains. "Part of me is thrilled to have my child home with me again. Another part of me wonders if I will ever truly know or understand this person who has come home wearing my child's body. She is definitely not the same girl I used to know. We have a lot of work to do to repair our broken relationship.

"And yet I know God is faithful. Through all this heartache, He kept my children safe. He has brought Maggie home to me, and I am confident that someday Steven will choose to come home again too. Meanwhile, I will continue to do what I've been doing all along—praying and standing on God's promises for my children.

"Although everyone else has been wonderful throughout this ordeal, God has been my mainstay, the One who has never forsaken me or my children, the One who will someday put us back together again as a family. Until that day, I will listen to and appreciate the advice I get from others, but ultimately I must rely on God every step of the way. In doing that, I have peace

125

in spite of the circumstances, because I know that God is greater than circumstances, and His promises to me and my family are true."

In the final analysis, then, after all the advice and input has been weighed and considered, our decisions and actions must be decided solely between ourselves and God if ever we are to have peace about our direction as we seek to restore our wandering children. As parents who love and desire to protect and rescue those children, we can settle for nothing less.

Chapter 10

Accountability

❖ Joe and Diane's fifteen-year-old daughter constantly criticized her parents for their commitment to
God and His Word. Her attitude was that they needed
God and the Bible to tell them what to do because they
were not strong enough to figure things out for themselves. Lost to her reasoning was the whole concept of
relationship, of caring for one another, and of the need
for fellowship with both God and other people. Her
eyes were blinded to how God made us to be and how
we are to relate to one another. Also void to her thinking was any knowledge of the fact that a very powerful
war is going on over the souls of men and women, and
that demons destroy people by destroying relationships through the doctrines they teach to men (see
1 Tim. 4:1).

We were not born with the knowledge of how to conduct ourselves responsibly toward other people. For the most part, these are learned responses. We must be taught to be kind, to be gentle, to be thankful. This is why Jesus taught as He did in the Sermon on the Mount (see Matt. 5).

Knowing Boundaries

Most of life is to be lived within boundaries. That means simply that there are limits on many things in life. The law of gravity limits how far we can jump. The law of audiodynamics limits how far our voices will carry. We learn to live with these natural laws. But there are other laws beyond these, laws of ethics and morality, which affect us much the way that natural laws do. Likewise, these laws cannot be broken without devastating consequences. If we violate the law of gravity by jumping off a twenty-story building, we will suffer grave consequences. The same is true with morality. Break one of these laws and you will ultimately pay the price.

For instance, adultery is breaking a law pertaining to marriage. God is not saying, "I don't want you to have fun or find fulfillment in life." God says, "I didn't create you to live this way; adultery won't work." Yet people persist in finding out for themselves and, in the process, destroy a beautiful part of life, usually winding up with a messed up marriage.

Accountability, then, deals with living within boundaries. Holding someone accountable is a form of love that says, "I care enough for you that I won't let you get hurt by going beyond the limits." Young people are not only protected in a household stressing accountability, they are loved. They may not understand this for a while, but consistency in loving discipline will eventually prove it.

One of the greatest disservices we can do for our children is to promote their rebellion by not enforcing the "house rules." Every home must have rules, and those in authority in the home must be the ones to set those rules. The parent support group Tough Love refers to this as "the *other* Golden Rule: He who has the gold rules." In other words, since you pay the bills and support your children, you have not only the right but the responsibility to set and enforce rules and guidelines for those living within your home And that includes everyone, no matter how old or how rebellious. From the time they are very young, children learn to pit parents, one against the other, in order to alter the rules. And they learn very quickly which rules will be enforced, and which can be stretched or even ignored. This game escalates as the children get older, especially when they come into their teenage years and are close to becoming adults.

If you have a house rule such as, "People who live in this house will not be involved in anything illegal," everyone—including and especially the rebellious young person—should know it beyond a shadow of a doubt. Should he or she choose to break that rule, and if repentance and restoration to an acceptable lifestyle

129

are not quickly forthcoming, your child should realize that he or she may no longer live in your home.

Explain Consequences

Sound drastic? It is. But drastic, destructive behavior requires drastic measures. If your child knows that you will stop short of removing him or her from the household, that child may well choose to ignore your other forms of correction and continue in his or her illegal and/or immoral lifestyle indefinitely. And you have just given over control of your home to someone living by the enemy's standards.

The ramifications of this sort of abdication are much more drastic than that of removing the rebellious young person from your home in an effort to see that child restored and the rest of your family preserved. Remember, however, that all such discipline must be carried out in a loving, controlled, and non-threatening manner.

While as parents we like to think that removing a child from our home is an option we will never have to consider—and for most of us, that's true—still, it must remain an option. Of course, that does not mean we can just turn a minor child out into the street. Legally and morally, we have a responsibility to provide food, clothing, shelter, and an education for our children until they are eighteen.

However, we are not required to do so within our own home. At times alternative living arrangements must be made for the sake of the child as well as the rest of the family. Although a child who has not become involved with the legal system cannot be turned over to the state, private schools or private foster care situations may be possible considerations. This sort of decision cannot be made without much prayer and counsel, and certainly not without pain, but under certain circumstances it may be the most loving and practical option available.

Face Your Responsibility

Parents make a big mistake when a child's rebellion begins to manifest itself in destructive behavior and the parents overlook it with the idea that it will go away. Because demons are behind the rebellion, they will seize parental passivity and use it to promote greater rebellion.

Many parents fail to teach their children accountability for their actions because they fear that discipline will drive them away, especially teenage children already displaying some independence. In truth, they may leave for a while, but loving discipline will eventually draw them back.

Demons are hindered by the laws of righteousness. They do not need to be commanded out of every situation. They leave when resisted through right acts. A parent holding his child responsible for his actions literally hinders the work of demons.

Two elements in deviate behavior need to be addressed. First is the action; second is the attitude. And often the action is a direct result of the attitude. In many cases the solution is to deal first with the action. In doing so, the attitude is often greatly changed. Actions are best dealt with through training. The Scripture is "Train a child," not "Teach a child" (Prov. 22:6). The difference comes through negatively in the statement, "Do as I say, not as I do." Accountability in children is only learned as parents commit to spending time with their children, modeling a life of accountability before them.

When Jerry wanted to work on his first car, his dad put on his work clothes, went out to the garage, and showed him what to do. Much of what Jerry learned throughout his lifetime came from watching his father. Any child who desires or needs to learn to do something will learn it best alongside a parent. Nowhere is that more obvious than when it comes to teaching our children the necessity of a personal relationship with the Lord.

If you, as a parent, do not have—and practice—a personal relationship with Jesus Christ, do not expect your children to do so. They will not accept it simply because you tell them it is important and send or even take them to church occasionally. Some young people today believe that "religion" is for little kids and old people. Really successful and "together" people have more important things to do. Where did they get that attitude? Television, music, books, sure—all those things contribute. But is it not possible that the primary contributor to that thinking is that they don't see a vital, ongoing, first-priority love relationship with Jesus in their parents?

Be honest. Do your children see you regularly spending time in Bible reading and prayer? Do they know that if the Super Bowl conflicts with Sunday service, you will tape the Super Bowl and watch it when you get home because spending time with God and with His people is more important to you than anything else? Do they see you talking and behaving one way in church, another way at home? The old adage "Actions speak louder than words" certainly applies when it comes to teaching your children. You are the authority in your home. Exercise that authority in a consistent, loving manner, both in word and in deed.

Because you are the authority in your home, attitudes characteristic of demon activity do not have to be tolerated within your sphere of authority, namely, your household. If you have determined that "as for me and my household, we will serve the Lord" (Josh. 24:15), then you do not have to allow a rebellious attitude to remain in your home.

Maintain Credibility

At this point many mistakes are made, especially if a parent is struggling with rejection, blame, or anger concerning the behavior of a child. It is all right to say, "This is my house and I refuse to let this evil attitude have control here." At the same time, remember that this is your child and all of his or her uniqueness still lies beneath this attitude change. Stay calm. Let patience run its course. Speak to both parts of the problem, the action as well as the attitude. Speak to the action by letting the person know the corresponding course of action you will take if things continue.

Ed and Ilene's fourteen-year-old daughter, Donna, persisted in running away. In some cases she was simply away without their permission. After trying every avenue they could think of to solve the problem, they finally decided that the next incident would result in police action. Donna was made aware of the consequence of any more rebellious behavior. But she persisted and was arrested when her dad called the police. She soon discovered that if her behavior continued, she would be made a ward of the court and a judge would determine what would happen to her.

Mary was faced with a similar situation with her son Rob. She had informed him in no uncertain terms that if she ever discovered drugs and/or drug paraphernalia in their home, she would immediately call the police. One morning, as she picked up some dirty clothes from his bedroom floor, she found what appeared to be a small amount of marijuana in a plastic bag. Mary was in agony. She knew what she had promised her son, and she knew what she must do. But her heart ached at the thought of reporting her own child to the authorities. And yet, knowing that she would damage her credibility beyond repair by not reporting her discovery, she called the police. Although no arrest was made due to the small amount of marijuana involved,

Rob was reminded that whatever his mother told him she would do in response to his behavior, she would indeed follow through on.

Some may wonder how Ed and Ilene or Mary could love their children and yet be willing to see them go to jail. Mary admits that she received some criticism for not "protecting her child." One friend even asked her if she wasn't afraid that Rob would feel betrayed and further withdraw from her. Rob's response, however, justified Mary's actions.

Mary, who works at home, was in her office next to her son's room the afternoon following her call to the police. She could overhear Rob on the phone, discussing the incident with a friend. From Rob's comments, it was obvious the friend had asked something to the effect of, "Aren't you mad at your mom for ratting on you?"

"Not really," Rob answered. "My mom always does what she says she's going to do. I should have believed her when she told me she'd call the police."

The question is not how Ed and Ilene or Mary could love their children and still turn them over to the police. The question is how some parents can say they love their children and yet protect their destructive behavior, creating the potential for more problems. Parents who really love their children will want to do everything possible to curtail destructive attitudes and activities, even if it means turning their children over to the proper authorities.

At the same time, note that Mary's response to Rob's

wrongdoing was carefully thought out. She had not arbitrarily warned Rob concerning her intended response to his actions without realizing she might have to do what she said she would do. A parent must never make a statement on which he or she cannot realistically follow through. If you have done that—given warnings in which your intended response is not in keeping with good discipline—you may have to apologize to your child and reorder your potential response. Idle and off-handed threats, as well as screaming and yelling or abusive physical punishment, only damage relationships.

Consider the Fallout of Rebellion

Holding our children accountable for their actions is not easy, because we too must be accountable to carry through with discipline. We cannot back down on proper training and discipline of our children, and we cannot allow ourselves to be intimidated by them. We are told of a visitor from another country who, after observing the American family for a time, commented, "Well, I must say, American parents certainly mind their children well." An unnerving observation, to say the least.

We cannot expect to raise accountable children if we are not first accountable parents. It is probably the most difficult job we will ever have, but to abdicate the responsibility is not only unfair to the rebellious child, but to all the others—and there are many—who are affected by the child's rebellion.

Maxine and George's oldest child's rebellion has almost destroyed the entire family. The girl's rebellion surfaced in her early teens and escalated throughout her high school years. From a straight-A student, the girl plummeted to barely passing, skipping school with friends, refusing to do homework, cursing and screaming and threatening anyone who tried to help or encourage her.

By the time the girl was sixteen, she had been arrested twice for drugs and placed on probation. Running away became her usual method of coping with any and all attempts by her parents to discipline her. She is now eighteen and living away from home in circumstances unknown to her family, showing up at home only to ask for money or other favors.

Sadly, the parents did not seek outside help until recently, when they began to see the "fallout" of their daughter's rebellion taking its toll on their other children, who have begun to copy their big sister's behavior. In addition, as a result of blaming themselves and each other, the parents' relationship is a shambles.

Only a miracle can pull this family back together now. Thankfully, God stands ready and able to perform miracles on our behalf, and to restore the years that rebellion has stolen (see Joel 2:25). But to see that miracle come to pass, we must first turn to Him with all our hearts, and then be ready to follow Him in loving obedience.

The fallout of rebellion can extend even beyond immediate family members. A rebellious teen can have a powerful impact not only on siblings but also on friends, either influencing the friends in his self-destructive direction, or turning them away from him entirely. The extended family—grandparents, cousins, aunts, uncles—is also affected.

In fact, none of the child's relationships will remain untouched. And although children may say they do not care whether others are hurt, deep down they are severely affected. When certain friends and even relatives avoid them, they know it is because of their behavior. They may attempt to rationalize that it is because those avoiding them are "nerds" and "losers," proclaiming loudly that they never liked them anyway. That sort of denial almost always indicates profound pain.

The child whose rebellious lifestyle causes "copycat" behavior in a younger sibling is usually pained beyond anything we can see or imagine. Although they may be willing to ignore or even defy the dangers of rebellion for themselves, most do not really want to see someone they love become involved in the same way.

And yet, admitting to their concern over those dangers would be to admit they have been wrong in what they have been arguing is right for so long. But the rebellious child's knowledge that a younger sibling has followed him or her into rebellion is a horrifying truth to deal with—and an even harder one to deny.

Richard will attest to that—at least, on his good days. Serving time in the mental ward of a youth prison, Richard knew that his younger brother, William, idolized him. When Richard started doing drugs and joined a gang, William wanted to join too.

"No way," Richard told him, time and again. "You stay in school and take care of Mom. You're too young for the streets."

But William didn't listen. He became what is known as a "wannabe," a kid hanging around a gang, dressing and talking and acting like them, hoping to be accepted. He was killed two days after his eleventh birthday by a rival gang during a drive-by shooting.

Richard went wild, killing two members of his rival gang and then turning the gun on himself. His physical injury has healed, but his mental prognosis is dim.

Their mother? She comes faithfully to the prison every Sunday to visit her living son, stopping along the way to leave flowers on the grave of her dead son. Talking to her about the situation is out of the question. The pain is just too great.

Will rebellious teens curb or even stop their behavior if made aware of their accountability and the extent of the possible fallout of their actions? Maybe. But whether they do or not, we must hold ourselves accountable to teach and train them. We cannot wait until our families are falling apart at the seams, or we are visiting our children in jail or in graves.

Help is available; our children will not seek it on their own, so we must do so immediately upon suspecting a problem. Rebellious teens must be told that, although they do not care now, the day will come when they will care again. By that time they will be carrying around so much fallout as a result of their behavior that they may never be totally free of its after-effects. Even if they do not believe what we tell them, they must see that *we* believe it. They must see that we hold ourselves accountable to get whatever help we can to prevent as much fallout as possible—for our rebellious children, for ourselves, and for the rest of our families.

And above all, our children must see that, because we are behaving in an accountable manner, we have a fallout shelter, and that shelter is Jesus Christ. In Him is hope, restoration, and healing. Run to Him and let Him protect you in the "shelter of the Most High" where "under his wings you will find refuge" (Ps. 91:1,4). Be accountable to stay there and continue to love and pray for that wandering one, and believe that, someday, your prodigal will join you.

Chapter 11

Dad and Mom on Trial

❖ Mavis and Clint had long suspected their son Fred was using drugs; however, they were never able to prove it, and both hoped they were wrong. When they came home unexpectedly and caught him smoking crack cocaine with two of his friends, their suspicions were drastically confirmed. In fact, the situation was worse than they had imagined. "Needless to say," Mavis explains, "we were shocked—devastated—when we were forced to move past the suspicion and face the fact that Fred was heavily involved in drugs. Part of me wanted to remain in denial, ignore the problem, and hope it would just go away. I realized it wouldn't, of course, and as responsible Christian parents, we had no choice but to face the problem head-on and deal with it, no matter how difficult the confrontation.

"Another part of me, however, was sure that the problem must somehow be my fault—or my husband's. Where had we gone wrong? Had we not loved Fred enough? Had we loved him too much? Been too restrictive, too indulgent? Thankfully, we realized that this line of thinking was certainly going to be of no help to Fred. And so we decided to forego the 'blame game' and focus on getting help for Fred.

"We were amazed, however, when we discussed the situation with his friends' parents, boys who were obviously as involved in drugs as Fred. One mother told us, 'My son tells me he is not on drugs, and that's good enough for me. Why snoop around and dig up trouble? He'll be grown and gone soon, and then I won't have to deal with it at all.' The other parents said, 'Yes, we've known about it for some time. But rather than make a big deal about it, we just tell him to do it in our garage where he'll be safe.'

"In the meantime, we knew we had to do everything we possibly could to save our son's life. We prayed, enlisted the prayers of others, learned as much as we could about drug use, detection, prevention, and treatment, working hand in hand with school officials and even the police as far as learning what we could and couldn't do legally. But in the end, it was between God and us. And the bottom line was we knew God held us accountable for what we permitted to go on within our home.

"After trying absolutely everything we could in an effort to stop Fred's self-destructive behavior—and getting nowhere—we knew that it was time to take the step that no parent ever wants to have to take. We had to inform our son that, since he was unwilling to give up his drug use or to stop associating with his current peer group, he could no longer live in our home.

"It was the most painful thing we have ever had to do. And yet, we knew that to allow this sin, this illegal, destructive behavior, to continue in our home, was to compound the sin, even sanctioning it. We would no longer be able to think of our home as a place that honors God. And when the day came that our son hit bottom and realized the enormity of the lie he had been living, there would be no truth for him to reach out to.

"And so we made other living arrangements for him. It's been a difficult adjustment, of course. But the most painful thing is knowing that he does not understand the kind of love that had no choice but to ask him to leave. He feels betrayed, abandoned for what he considers 'no good reason.' In his immaturity and deception, he believes we are the ones at fault, the ones who betrayed him. He does not see his own sin, or the pain he has caused the rest of his family.

"And yet we are confident that someday he will. Until then, we have to stand strong in what we believe is the right thing to do in our particular situation. We must let him know that we love him unconditionally—whether he believes us now or not—but we must also let him know that we will not accept nor condone his illegal or immoral behavior. We have also let him know that, when he is ready for help, ready to leave his current lifestyle behind, we will be here for him. That's the kind of love God requires of us as parents, because it's the kind of love He offers to us as His children."

Mavis and Clint were wise in focusing on the immediate problem rather than getting sucked into the "blame game," as they called it. And yet, are parents not in part responsible for children's actions and behavior and choices?

Biblical Commands

God's Word speaks both to children and to parents regarding our responsibilities toward each other. To a child God says, "Children, obey your parents in the Lord, for this is right. 'Honor your father and mother'—which is the first commandment with a promise—'that it may go well with you and that you may enjoy long life on the earth'" (Eph. 6:1-3). To parents God says, "Fathers, do not exasperate your children; instead, bring them up in the training and instruction of the Lord" (Eph. 6:4).

Whatever you choose for the ABC's of raising your children, make sure you use a biblical model. Give them sound counsel and instruction. Be prepared to lovingly but firmly deal with problems—even suspected problems—in your children's lives as soon as they crop up. To ignore those problems, as Fred's friends' parents chose to do, is abdicating your responsibilities as parents and will not help your children solve their problems.

We may rationalize that we need to support our children, even in their sin. But supporting sin is sin itself and will not minimize the destructive outcome of rebellious behavior. Sin added to sin minimizes nothing; it only adds to the problem by refusing a head-on confrontation with error. Such confrontation does not have to be nasty. It simply needs to lovingly carry the conviction of right and wrong, not in some self-styled legalistic way, but in keeping with what is correct according to the Scriptures.

Beyond the formal training of a child, a parent must understand that much of what a child learns is not taught but caught. He or she learns by what is modeled. The sin we allow in moderation, they may allow in excess.

Many parents would do almost anything to see that their children get a good education. When possible, college funds are set aside early in children's lives so that they may continue their education after high school. We trust that their education will positively influence their lives in the future.

Our Examples

But what about the silent education that goes on every day in our households, the kind that is modeled by example? If we are positive and upbeat, the chances are increased that our children will, to some degree, be the same way. If, on the other hand, we are bitter and critical, our children have a greater likelihood of picking up those same traits. Even if a child learns to hate the negativeness found in a parent, the chances that the enemy of his soul will endeavor to make him the same way are extremely high. Exposure to negative attitudes, if not checked and resisted, will duplicate or even multiply themselves in our children.

You may have made a lot of mistakes in the past and perhaps now see how wrong you were. Don't despair—and don't get drawn into playing the "blame game." Begin a road to recovery and blessing by first admitting to God that you were wrong. Then tell your children what you are learning. Tell them that you are sorry for your actions in the past and, with God's help, things will be different in the future. Apologizing to your children for mistakes you have made will endear you to them if done correctly.

The life we live before our children will have a monumental effect upon them. But the life we live behind the scenes will also affect them. We may rationalize that our private life is nobody's business but our own, but this simply is not true. All wrongdoing will eventually be exposed. Jesus said, "There is nothing concealed that will not be disclosed, or hidden that will not be made known" (Luke 12:2). And when your kids find out, apart from your confession and turning from your sin, you may open a door for the enemy to do something similar or worse in them.

Being aware of what negative influences can do to our children is only half the problem. The other half is learning to put positive influences in them. And nothing is more important in this area than learning to spend time with them.

RAY'S STORY_____

Our kids aren't perfect, but Linda and I are proud of all four of them. They have their problems and we aren't assured that they will not have more. One reason we believe they are doing well is that we spend vast amounts of time with them. Sports, shopping, playing games, talking, working together on projects—all contribute to our closeness and all contribute to the kind of influence they will need to counter ungodly influence from the world.

The most important influence, however, comes from our worshipping together. We rally around this point. Our church has become a central part of the influence we want them to have. We feel so strongly about how our kids relate to a church atmosphere that we are willing to change churches if need be to provide them a place where they can better grow in the Lord. For a number of years we've enjoyed having our kids excited about going to church.

_____ ◆

KATHI'S STORY_____

I never cease to be amazed at the memories that stand out most in children's minds. Like many parents, we've tried to incorporate a variety of activities and learning experiences into our family life, including trips to Disneyland, museums, church camping trips, and even vacations to other parts of the country. And although I'm sure those excursions are remembered and appreciated, it seems to be what we often think of as the "little things" that are most vivid in our children's memories: the soccer game where we sat through the rain and watched our son's team go down in defeat and then went out for a consolation pizza afterward; sitting scrunched up together on the couch and watching the Muppet movie on TV while we ate popcorn; going out to brunch after church on Sunday mornings.

If we've learned anything through reviewing our family's favorite memories, it's that developing relationships with our children takes time and energy, but it's time and energy well spent. Although we may still be waiting to reap some of the rewards of those years invested in child rearing, Larry and I are confident that God will use those precious memories to help turn our son's heart toward home once again.

---------- ♦

Invest Your Time

Both quantity and quality of time spent with our children are important. Quantity is primarily determined by work and school schedules. Quality, however, is something we can engineer on our own. Draw your children into your own experiences every chance you get. Do you like to fish? Take them with you. If you find they don't enjoy it, try something else. Maybe an afternoon at the mall is more appealing to them.

Whatever it may be, find something you can do together, and then do it—often. Between giving our children insights into our own interests and discovering the things they delight in, we can build a bond that will help drown out the potentially devastating voices of the world.

Sadly, many parents and teens or preteens spend little or almost no time together. Little has been done in the child's younger years to cultivate common interests, and now neither is willing to bend in order to accommodate the other. Consequently, their lives move in completely opposite directions. The common parental lament becomes, "I just don't know my child anymore," while the child complains, "My parents just don't understand me." Unfortunately, both of them are right. A parent and child cannot communicate meaningfully if they don't spend time together. And it follows that we cannot know or understand someone with whom we don't communicate.

On the other hand, if we spend too much time with our children, we may become overly involved with their lives. We can become so wrapped up in them that we try to control and smother them, seeing them as extensions of ourselves rather than the unique individuals they are. Although this overprotectiveness may be born out of a deep love for them, we actually harm them by trying to relive our own lives through them.

For instance, a father who spent his growing up years with baby-sitters may decide early on that his child will never be left in the care of a stranger. Instead, he insists on spending every spare moment with his own son, going everywhere with him, even when his son is perfectly capable of doing things on his own. A mother, on the other hand, who grew up in poverty may have a burning desire to try to buy her children happiness, giving them things they neither need nor want. Another father who never made it at professional sports may insist that his son is going to play for a major baseball team some day, whether he wants to or not. Every spare moment is spent pitching a baseball back and forth between them, when what the child really wants is to read a book or do something else with his dad.

To some degree, most parents are guilty of this vicarious living. We want to be our children's problem solvers. Psychologists refer to this as "enabling." However, by running interference for our children at every turn of the road, we deny them the maturity that comes only by walking through a problem and coming out on the other side.

Being wrapped up in our children's lives is nothing new. From the dawn of time, first-time mothers and fathers have learned that, once you lay eyes on your tiny miracle from God, you are never the same. God meant it to be so. But He also meant for us to spend time during our children's young years teaching them how to properly let go of us and go out and stand on their own. The problem is, we become like the great patriarch Jacob, whose "life [was] closely bound up with the boy's [Benjamin's] life" (see Gen. 44:30), so much so that his other sons feared their father would die if anything happened to Benjamin.

Communicate Effectively

Other parents complain that, even though they want to spend quality time communicating with their children, it is impossible because the child "will not talk to me." Sometimes the problem is not so much that the child won't talk to the parent, it's that the parent's attempts at initiating a conversation are awkward and unnatural.

Few parents are equipped to be professional counselors. To sit a child down for the dreaded "family conference" and expect them to open up about their innermost thoughts and feelings is fatal to effective communication. It is much more natural for a child to open up during a one-on-one game of shooting hoops with Dad or a leisurely day spent at the mall with Mom. The best communication times with our children often happen as a natural outflow of fun activities together.

Although not always the case, sometimes children won't talk to parents because of what we will refer to as "defensive shut-down." It begins in early childhood, escalating to a dangerously sensitive level in preadolescence, when children's opinions of themselves are at their most fragile state. Thoughtless parents, often in a poor attempt to discipline, attack the child rather than the problem by making cutting remarks that may brand a child for life.

"You're so lazy!" bellows the angry father, who comes home to discover his ten-year-old son has yet to mow the lawn. "You'll never amount to anything."

"You're just stupid," exclaims the exasperated mother, staring at her daughter's math grade. "I'd hire a tutor, but it's no use. You're hopeless."

"You'd better not eat that ice cream," warns the chubby twelve-year-old's mother. "You'll never get a boyfriend with a figure like that!"

The already insecure child has just been tried and convicted, pronounced worthless by the one authority figure who knows him or her better than anyone else. In self-defense, the child shuts down, shuts up, and quits trying. In later years, the parent wonders why it is that the child has turned to an unsavory peer group, talking to newfound friends for hours on end, while at home having little or nothing to say.

We are not implying that every child who turns to a peer group for companionship does so through some communication fault of the parent. But we must measure our words carefully, using them to build up and encourage, rather than tear down and discourage, if we expect to raise healthy, communicative offspring. Life is tough enough without being verbally declared a loser by our parents.

Looking back at the above illustrations, how better could these parents have handled these situations with their children? Perhaps the irate father who came home to find the lawn still unmowed—after having reminded his son several times before leaving the house—could have avoided the angry confrontation by being more specific about his requirements before leaving home.

"Son, I'm going to town for a couple of hours. When I return, I expect to find the lawn mowed. If it's not, there will be no ball game this weekend."

Simple and to the point. And then, before walking away, the father could have asked his son to repeat what he has said to be sure there is no misunderstanding. The key, of course, is when Dad gets home and the lawn isn't mowed. Then he need not yell, but he must follow through on his promise of no ball game.

In the case of the exasperated mother whose daughter has received a poor grade in math, the first thing to consider is, does the child have the ability to do better? If a child is capable of nothing more than a C+, that child should be applauded for a C+ as surely as if it were an A. But suppose the child is easily capable of an A and yet has brought home a C+. Is the child being rebellious by refusing to do what is required of her? Then she should be corrected accordingly. Is her rebellion being fueled by a negative peer influence, drugs, alcohol, sexual activity? A wise parent will seek to deal with the root problem before it gets worse. Labeling a child as "stupid" will do nothing to alleviate the problem; it will, in fact, exacerbate it.

As for the chubby twelve-year-old whose mother is concerned that she is overeating, many factors need to be considered here. First and foremost, no one should be attacked for the way he or she looks. Poking fun at someone's height or weight or hair color or facial and body features is inexcusable. At the same time, if a parent is truly concerned about the child's weight being unhealthy, the child should be checked by a doctor. Some children go through what is commonly known as a "baby fat" stage, only to stretch out and lose that a couple of years later. In addition, body shape and size are governed, to a large degree, by heredity.

Use Appropriate Discipline

Finally, although we have alluded to this problem before, no chapter about moms and dads on trial would be complete without another strong admonition against distorting or perverting parental authority and responsibility to abuse our children in any way. If you know or even suspect that your treatment of your child constitutes physical, emotional, or sexual abuse, get help immediately. Consult a trusted pastor, physician, friend, or even a parent support group for the help you need so that you, in turn, can help your child receive healing and restoration.

Remember, God's Word to us as parents is not to provoke our children to anger so that they become discouraged (see Col. 3:21). We are not to create hostility in them.

God is warning us not to treat our children in such a way as to produce a deadly or fatal reaction. Instead, we are to "bring them up in the training and instruction of the Lord." We must raise them according to biblical guidelines, doing everything possible to keep or deliver them from sin. We must also do so with huge amounts of unconditional love, being careful to encourage and build them up, assuring them that their home is a safe haven from a world that in many ways would do its best to tear them down.

Then, even if they should choose to prematurely leave that safe haven someday, they will know where to run when the deceitful lure of the world exposes itself for the cheap imitation that it is. When the enemy's lies have left them empty and alone, they can come home to the truth that will finally make them free. And you, as a parent, will be free of the "blame game," knowing you have searched your heart, asked forgiveness for the mistakes you may have made while raising your children, and sought restoration wherever possible.

Chapter 12

Legal Implications

❖ Jeanie, a single mother of three, received a phone call one Friday afternoon, informing her that Child Protective Services would be at her home on Saturday morning to remove Jeanie's oldest child from her custody. Flabbergasted, Jeanie demanded an explanation.

"We have received a report of child abuse," the woman replied.

"Against me?" asked Jeanie.

"Yes," answered the woman.

No further explanation was forthcoming. In the case of alleged child abuse, none is required before removing the child from the home—not even the specifics of the accusations. Unlike any other crime in which the defendant is considered innocent until proven guilty, in most cases those accused of child abuse are treated as if guilty until proven innocent. The accused is not entitled to confront or even to know the identity of the accuser. Only as the case moves through the courts does the accused even learn the specifics of the accusations.

The entire burden of proof falls on the accused, along with the devastation of having a child forcibly removed from the home and the ensuing ruination of the accused's reputation. Although we are in full agreement that child abuse is an abhorrent crime and that laws must protect innocent children—as our current laws were set up to do—we believe some of those laws have been carried to extremes and do not have enough built-in safeguards to protect the family unit, as Jeanie's case so clearly illustrates.

False Accusations

Jeanie is still in the midst of her nightmare, being denied access to her child, as well as being terrified that the same agency may come and take her other two children from her. With little money to wage an expensive court battle, she is at a loss as to what to do next.

Unfortunately, Jeanie's story is not an isolated one. In fact, this all-too-familiar story strikes terror into the hearts of many parents, especially those with rebellious teens. Because the identity of those making accusations of suspected child abuse must be kept confidential, an angry and rebellious child can easily report his or her parents for child abuse, either as an act of retaliation or in a foolish attempt to get away from what the child considers unreasonable rules and regulations. Sadly, the child who believes this call will either result in the parents "lightening up" on those rules and regulations or the child's being placed in a foster home situation where there are no such restrictions is in for a rude awakening.

Almost without exception, this sort of action on the part of a defiant and rebellious child results in the child's removal from the home (and possibly the removal of other children in the family as well) and placement in a situation where the rules and regulations may be much more stringent than anything previously experienced. In addition, these new restrictions will be administered without benefit of parental love and concern.

This is why your children must know that you will not be blackmailed or threatened into backing down on what you believe is right. And in the unlikely event that your child threatens legal action, you need to stress to him or her that to make a false accusation of child abuse will cause long-term pain to everyone in the family, including and especially the child making the report. Often children, especially when angry, do not think beyond the immediate situation and their need to strike back at their parents. Your child must know that a call to a child protective services agency will more than likely result in the child's being placed in a situation where he or she has less freedom than before. The child cannot simply change his or her mind and return home once regret over the hasty action sets in. These two facts may be enough to stop the child from any such foolish action.

Besides making your child aware of the monumental ramifications of such an accusation, keep in mind another very important fact. Whoever it is that may decide to make a false accusation of child abuse against you, whether it be your rebellious teen, an angry neighbor, or a vengeful spouse, the consequences may very well go beyond the removal of the child from your home. Depending on the severity of the charge, you could be prosecuted and even end up serving a jail sentence if you are unable to prove your innocence.

When denied the constitutional rights afforded to those accused of any other crime—such as the right to confront your accusers, to see the bills of particulars (stating the alleged offense), and the right to copy records (agency created records may be withheld because of confidentiality)—proving your innocence is not an easy undertaking. In addition, parents may be billed for medical examinations, therapy, and child support. This is true, even if the child is removed from your home at your request, and is made a ward of the court as explained earlier.

To further compound the lack of justice in alleged child abuse cases, "professional" perverts and/or pedophiles, as well as some truly abusive parents, know how to play the system. Through the use of well-versed lawyers, coupled with so-called cooperation and plea bargaining, many of these child abusers are released with little more than a slap on the wrist. Yet a wrongly accused parent must endure the loss of a child (and possibly all children), loss of reputation, possible loss of a job, and possible jail time.

Thankfully, resources for falsely accused parents have sprung up across the country, one of the better known being the National Child Abuse Defense & Resource Center.[1]

Beyond the legal ramifications of this sort of situation, note that Ephesians 6:12 is still our mainstay of truth: "For our struggle is not against flesh and blood, but against the rulers, against the authorities, against the powers of this dark world and against the spiritual forces of evil in the heavenly realms." God is the One who established the family unit; therefore, Satan hates families and will stop at nothing to destroy them. Rebellion is demonic in origin. A child who makes a false child abuse report against a parent may very well be operating under demonic influence, as Jeanie will readily attest.

"I couldn't believe it," she sobbed, as tears trickled down her cheeks. "I couldn't imagine who it was that would make such an ugly and false accusation, and then I found out it was my own child! He lied about me and said I had been abusing him. True, we hadn't been getting along well, ever since he hit his teens and turned rebellious. The more rebellious he became, the harder I came down on him. I didn't know what else to do! But I certainly never abused him in any way.

"When they came to take him away and I asked

them who it was that had reported me, they wouldn't tell me," Jeanie went on. "But one look in my son's defiant eyes as they led him out the door, and I knew. When I began to cry and ask him why he had done it, he just laughed. It was the most evil sound I have ever heard. It was not my son's laugh. And it was not his voice that informed me, 'I never want to see you again. I wish you were dead.'"

Clear Responsibility

Again, although the laws regarding alleged child abuse may sometimes seem unfair, the devil is our enemy, not the legal system itself. In many instances, that legal system can be our ally, particularly if a child has become such a problem that allowing him or her to remain in the home any longer could become a threat—either physically, emotionally, or spiritually—to the rest of the family. Countless officials, working within the legal system as lawyers, probation officers, policemen, judges, or counselors, truly care for our children and want what is best for them. Unfortunately, the vast number of juvenile cases prevent many of them from taking a personal interest in the children involved.

This, of course, is all the more reason why we must educate ourselves as to our legal rights and responsibilities. One of the heaviest of these responsibilities is that we can be held accountable for many of the illegal things our children do.

For instance, if you suspect your child may be deal

ing drugs from your home, you absolutely cannot afford to ignore that suspicion. Parent support groups teach that, regardless of whether or not you have concrete evidence, if you suspect your child is using drugs, he probably is; if you suspect he is dealing drugs, he probably is; if you suspect he is involved with gangs, he probably is. The moment you choose to ignore that suspicion, you become an accomplice to your child's crime, as well as to his own possible destruction.

Let us explain. If, as we said, you suspect your child is involved in dealing drugs from your home, he probably is. And you, undoubtedly, have detected signs that caused you to entertain this suspicion: strange and often brief phone calls at all hours, including "hang ups" when you answer, followed by your child's leaving the home or someone showing up for a quick, secretive meeting; slits in the screen on your child's bedroom window through which small amounts of drugs and cash can be passed; slips of paper in your child's room, listing first names of people you don't know, followed by unexplained numbers; a "beeper" that your child suddenly acquires. Any of these signs point to probable drug dealing or gang involvement.

If you fail to do everything within your power at that point—prayer, counseling, legal advice—you have set yourself up to lose everything you own—including your child. How? Based on forfeiture laws in many states as well as similar federal statutes, any property used in illegal activity is subject to seizure by authorities. If you have noticed signs of drug dealing in your home, you may not be the only one with suspicions. Sooner or later, your child is going to be arrested, and if it can be proven that he or she was dealing drugs from your home, you may be subject to losing that home, as well as many of your other assets.

Over and above the legal implications of ignoring your child's suspected criminal activity, what about the moral implications? From the time you suspect such activity and refuse to act on it, you are every bit as guilty as your child—if not more so—each time someone else uses one of the illegal, destructive, and potentially deadly drugs that has been sold to them by your child. Your child's sin has just become your sin.

One common excuse heard at parent support group meetings comes from parents who suspect something illegal and/or immoral is going on with their child. Because they falsely believe the lie that their child has an irrevocable right to privacy, the parent does not search the child's room. True, every individual has a right to a certain amount of privacy, but when that individual chooses to break the rules—whether they be rules of the house or rules of the legal system—the right to privacy is forfeited. Those in charge have the responsibility to investigate and do whatever is necessary to see that those rules are no longer broken.

This is not an excuse to snoop through your child's belongings because you are curious. If there are no real indications that your child is involved in questionable activity, you may do more harm than good with your false suspicions. The rule is to go slowly and exercise patience and not let the enemy put false suspicions in your mind.

RAY'S STORY_____

I feel no necessity to eavesdrop or search either of our girl's rooms at present. I hope I never have to. The reason is that we have good communication and I want them to feel that our home is their home. They have a say in what goes on here because we have a relationship that is void of defiance and other kinds of rebellion. If that relationship ever changes, however, my responsibility as a parent would change from respecting our child's privacy to doing whatever is necessary to rescue that child from the consequences of rebellion.

_____ ♦

KATHI'S STORY_____

That is exactly what happened in our case with our youngest son, Chris. In his earlier years, we would never have dreamed of going into his room and going through his private things. In fact, since he was a little boy, Chris has been a pack rat. He saves everything, from last year's Christmas cards to his favorite childhood toys. And we've always respected that and left his things alone. But when we finally realized that Chris was becoming more and more involved in destructive behavior, we felt we had no choice but to do everything possible to intervene before it was too late. Periodic room searches became an unwelcome part of our lives.

———————————————————————— ◆

Forfeiture of Rights

When someone is arrested for a crime, he or she has just forfeited several rights, one of those being the right to privacy. When we first suspect problems with a child, we should communicate with that child on every aspect of the situation. As lovingly and firmly as possible, we must inform the child that, although we want to trust him or her and continue to respect his or her privacy, if the questionable behavior continues, that may no longer be possible.

If the behavior continues and our suspicions of illegal activities deepen, we must take the initiative and conduct a "search and seizure" of the child's room. This is tough, but as responsible parents, we have no choice. The child will undoubtedly be furious, screaming "you have no right to come into my room and go through my things." At that point, we need to calmly remind the child that it is not his or her room, but a room in our home which we allow him or her to use. Remembering this avoids uncertainties as to how to deal with teens who choose to cover their bedroom walls with immoral or demonic posters. The minute they violate the house rules, we must hold them to the consequences. We cannot afford to compromise on this point.

Should you decide your child needs more help than

you can give, your legal rights may be somewhat limited. For instance, although you can have your minor child committed to a treatment or rehabilitation center against his or her will, you can only do so if that commitment is endorsed by one of the center's attending physicians. If the center where you wish to place your child does not have psychiatric or psychological care, then no matter how high a success rate the organization may have, your child must sign in voluntarily. These limitations are nationwide.

This is a sad situation, since some organizations designed to help troubled teens operate apart from psychiatric and psychological programs and do so with very high success rates. Teen Challenge, for instance, is a Christ-centered organization funded strictly by donations, and has a phenomenal success rate of 86 percent, meaning that graduates stay alcohol-and drug-free for at least five years after completing the program. This rate is anywhere from three to ten times as high as many treatment and rehabilitation centers with expensive psychiatric and psychological programs. Unfortunately, Teen Challenge can only accept teens who voluntarily commit to the program. A rebellious teen is probably going to have to hit rock bottom before agreeing to check into a place like Teen Challenge.

This should not alarm you, but rather encourage you to be educated about the legal system and involved to whatever degree necessary when you suspect your child is participating in illegal and/or immoral behavior. Avoiding the problem will accomplish nothing. Remember who our real enemy is—the demonic realm—and pray accordingly. That is our first and most important line of defense. Legal preparation is another vital step we can take to rescue our children and to protect ourselves and the rest of our families.

Do not wait until you find yourself in a position like Jeanie's with Child Protective Services agents at your door, ready to remove your rebellious teen from your home. Act now—contact a parent support group or the parents' rights group listed in the notes for this chapter and learn about your legal rights, responsibilities, options, and limitations—before you face the possibility of dealing with the legal system. That ounce of prevention now could easily be worth so much more than a pound of cure later.

Chapter 13

Praying for Our Children

❖ This book has been about rebellion, about deception, about the need for tough-love discipline, about effective communication, and about the absolute necessity to do warfare in the spiritual realm. Now let us get specific about some practical how-to's of that spiritual warfare.

Although waging war in the spiritual realm is very serious business, it need not be intimidating. The first and most important requirement for becoming involved in spiritual warfare is personally being forgiven and cleansed by the blood of Jesus Christ, and walking in close communion with and obedience to God. Unfortunately, thousands of people are saved and yet are not walking closely to Him. They are converts, not disciples.

Disciples are those who walk in daily communion with God, following Him obediently wherever He leads. If and when they allow sin to enter their lives, they immediately repent and receive forgiveness and cleansing (see 1 John 1:9) and then move ahead in their relationship with Him. Discipleship is the prerequisite for becoming a mighty warrior in God's army, and this requirement is not met without ongoing, committed effort.

At the same time, we cannot earn our right to be disciples, anymore than we can earn our right to be converts. It is all by God's grace and by the finished work of Jesus Christ at Calvary. But we must appropriate that grace and that finished work through prayer, Bible reading and study, praise and worship, and corporate gathering with other believers. There simply is no other way to grow in our relationship with the Lord. And if we are not growing, we are not going to be effective prayer warriors.

Spiritual warfare is more than a defensive measure to repel the enemy's attacks; it is an offensive strategy for advancing the kingdom of God and taking back territory the enemy has laid claim to—in this case, your rebellious child.

True, your child has a right to rebel and choose to walk away from God, but you have a right and a responsibility to stand on God's Word and fight. Remind the demonic hordes that they have no claim to your family because you are a believer in Jesus Christ, for the Bible promises not only your own salvation, but the eventual salvation of your household as well (see Acts 16:31).

The toughest word in the previous sentence is the word _eventual_. As members of the "instant generation," if we cannot microwave it, we don't want it. But spiritual warfare requires patience and perseverance. Soldiers who desert because the fighting is too fierce and the battle too long are considered AWOL. The saddest thing is that deserters will never know the victory that may have awaited them just around the next corner.

Armed for the Battle

But even if you have only recently enlisted in God's army, or if you enlisted some years ago and then went AWOL, or maybe you did not fight because you did not realize there was a war going on—you can start now. God has not disqualified you for future combat. All willing warriors are readily received and restored and mightily used, for God's desire is that all His children enjoy the fruits of victory.

So no matter how long or how fierce your battle has been or continues to be, _don't give up!_ Because the enemy knows he is outmatched and because his basic weapon is deception, he uses that deception to "wear out the saints" (see Dan. 7:25, KJV). "Why don't you just give up?" he whispers. "You've been praying for years and nothing has changed. In fact, ever since you started praying, things have gotten worse. It's hopeless Hopeless. Hopeless. . " That word echoes

171

through your mind until you are "worn out" from the fight. But remember, everything the enemy tells you is a lie. Jesus said of the devil, "There is no truth in him. . . . [F]or he is a liar and the father of lies" (John 8:44).

As warriors, we must stand strong and resist the enemy. When the enemy comes at you with his lies, trying to discourage you and get you to back down from the fight, the disciple (one who is yielded and submitted to God's will for his or her life, growing and becoming stronger through daily communion with Him) can resist and defeat the devil's lies by counterattacking with the truth of God's Word. For instance, if the devil is trying to convince you that your child will never turn away from his or her destructive lifestyle and return to God and to the rest of the family, you can resist that lie with the following Scriptures:

> Believe in the Lord Jesus, and you will be saved—you and your household.
>
> (Acts 16:31)

> I will contend with those who contend with you, and your children I will save.
>
> (Isa. 49:25)

> "Restrain your voice from weeping and your eyes from tears, for your work will be rewarded," declares the LORD. "They will return from the land of the enemy. So there is hope for your future," declares the LORD. "Your children will return to their own land."
>
> (Jer. 31:16–17)

Many more scriptures can help you stand when doing battle with the enemy for the souls of your children. You can discover them through your own Bible reading and then appropriate them into your life by repeating them aloud daily, particularly when you sense the enemy's hot breath on the back of your neck. Romans 10:17 tells us that "faith comes by hearing, and hearing by the word of God" (NKJV).

By continually *speaking* the Word of God out loud, we *hear* it in our hearts and, therefore, our faith grows. Even the most miraculous signs from heaven will not increase or sustain faith within someone who is not continually hearing the Word of God. Read it. Speak it. Listen to it. And then, when the enemy comes with his lies, the truth of God's Word will rise up in you and you will cut down your adversary with one mighty slash of the Word of God, referred to as "the sword of the Spirit" (Ephesians 6:17).

That sword of the Spirit is given to us to do battle, both offensively and defensively, against the enemy of our souls—and the enemy of our children's souls. In fact, much of the sixth chapter of Ephesians is devoted to explaining how to put on the "full armor of God" (v. 11), an explanation and a command we cannot afford to ignore if we desire to be victorious over the devil.

Satan is a formidable foe if we are not clothed in God's armor. This armor consists of the belt of truth (see John 14:6); the breastplate of righteousness (see Rom 10:4); feet fitted with the readiness that comes from the gospel of peace (see Is. 52:7); the shield of faith (see Rom. 10:17); the helmet of salvation (see Rom. 10:9–10); and the sword of the Spirit (see Luke 4:1–13). Armed and covered in this way, the enemy *cannot* defeat us.

Prayer

Ephesians 6 instructs us to "pray in the Spirit on all occasions with all kinds of prayers and requests." Although there may be some controversy over the type of prayers referred to here, one thing is certain, all means *all*. We must persevere in prayer, taking all our requests to the throne of God, seeking God on our own as well as with others, remaining in a constant readiness to pray, and doing so by whatever means God has made available to us.

One of those means—and without a doubt, one of the most powerful—is to petition God in our own "prayer language." A thorough study of the Book of Acts, as well as other New Testament passages, reveals that praying in an unknown language or in "other tongues" (see Acts 2:4; 10:46; 19:6; Rom 8:26–27; 1 Cor. 14:14–18, 39) is a valid means of intercession and of speaking to God. Although we do not desire to get into a lengthy discourse on the subject, we encourage those of you who have already received your prayer language to use it often when you are involved in spiritual warfare, remembering that the enemy cannot "decode" this type of prayer. If you have never prayed in this manner but would like to, the two most important things to remember are that you must first be born again; and second, you are simply seeking the fullness of the Holy Spirit (see Acts 19:1–6). This is not necessary for salvation. It is simply an enablement for power.

When we are engaged in warfare for our children— or anyone else, for that matter—two primary types of prayer are involved: first, interceding before the Father in Jesus' name; second, speaking to demons in Jesus' name. Here is a sample prayer you can use in speaking to the Father, combining petitions to Him as well as declarations of the truth of Scripture:

> *Father, Your Word says that children are a heritage from the Lord. I thank You, Lord, for the heritage You've given me in my children. And Father, Your Word also says that if I will delight myself in You, You will give me the desires of my heart.*
>
> *Lord, you know that I delight myself in You, and You know the desire of my heart regarding my children, which is that they walk in Your truth. Father, I know that my cries unto you are not in vain. Bring my children into Yourself and restore them unto their family and those who love them.*
>
> *Lord, You are my Hope. I will rest in that hope because your Word has promised to heal my children, to lead them, and to restore comforts to them and their mourners.*
>
> *Father, I believe Your Word, which assures me that all my children shall be taught by You and shall have great peace. I thank You that You are the One who*

contends with those who contend with me and You save my children.

Lord, by the power of Your grace, I commit myself to Your Word, which tells me to be careful to seek to walk in Your ways that I may possess this good land and leave it as an inheritance for my children after me forever.

I thank You, Lord, that You are faithful to watch over Your Word to perform it, and I thank You for the good land You have given to me and to my children after me forever. In Jesus' mighty name. Amen.

Although praying this prayer as it is written is both powerful and beneficial, we encourage you to study it and then pray a similar prayer in your own words, based on Scriptures you have found especially meaningful to you.

Praise and Worship

One of the most powerful weapons in our arsenal is praise and worship. Because praise and worship are directed toward God and because He promises to inhabit the praises of His people (see Ps. 22:3), this weapon is extremely powerful against the enemy of our soul. To praise and worship God is to invite the overflow of His very presence upon and within You. What could possibly be more intimidating to Satan!

Israel knew this. When they went into battle against the men of Ammon, Moab, and Mount Seir, praisers and worshippers went out before the soldiers (see 2 Chron. 20:22). They knew they were not strong enough to defeat the enemy in their own strength, but they believed that God's presence would bring them the victory.

That is why it is so important, especially when engaging in spiritual warfare, to be people of praise and worship. Walking through your home while singing aloud to God can, in and of itself, cause demon spirits to flee the premises. Although you may feel strange doing this the first few times, remember that the enemy will try to intimidate you into quitting. If he can appeal to your pride—"How ridiculous you look! Wouldn't you be embarrassed if someone saw you!"— he will certainly do so. Don't give in to him. Once you have made praise and worship a regular part of your everyday life, you will wonder how you ever got along without it.

One common problem expressed by those sincerely trying to build a strong and consistent prayer life is that, as soon as they sit down (or lie or kneel or stand) to pray, their mind begins to wander, or else it goes blank and they can't think of a thing to say. You may find these suggestions helpful:

- Write your prayers in a journal. This not only helps you stay focused while praying, you also can go back to record God's faithfulness in answering your prayers.
- Pray the Scriptures, especially the Psalms. There's nothing more encouraging than to speak out the great words of faith found in the book of Psalms,

many of them written during times of tremendous hardship and trials.

- Pray in your prayer language.
- Find a prayer partner, someone you can call in emergencies, and to whom you will be accountable to meet and pray with on a regular basis.
- Pray for specifics in your children's lives: the pursuit of righteousness; a zeal for God; wholesome friends and relationships; strength to withstand temptation; a desire to adopt biblical values; a strong personal relationship with Jesus, which will enable them to make wise choices and decisions on their own.

Warfare Prayer

Addressing demons in Jesus' Name—warfare praying—seldom resembles the Hollywood-type scenes portrayed in such movies as "The Exorcist." Although on occasion demons may put up quite a fight when ordered in the name of Jesus to leave someone, it does not always happen that way.

Before repossessing that which the enemy has taken, Jesus said we must first "tie up [bind] the strong man" (Matt. 12:29). Later Jesus further explains that "whatever you bind on earth will be bound in heaven, and whatever you loose on earth will be loosed in heaven" (Matt. 18:18).

This means that we can speak directly to the spirits of darkness who are influencing our children and command them in the name of Jesus to take their hands off them. If we have discerned that our child is being influenced by a spirit of rebellion, we may come against that spirit by saying, "In the name of Jesus, I bind you, spirit of rebellion, and I command you to loose my child and to cease your harassment and influence over him immediately." Any such command issued by a disciple of Jesus Christ must be obeyed. But, even if your child has been loosed from the spirit of rebellion, that child can voluntarily or involuntarily invite him back. The child does not have to speak to a spirit of rebellion and verbally invite it back into his life. He can do so nonverbally through decisions and actions of his own. By choosing to continue in a rebellious lifestyle, the spirit of rebellion may very well return.

In fact, the Scripture warns that, once a demon has been ordered out of someone, if that person doesn't immediately give his or her heart to Christ so that the Holy Spirit can come and dwell within, the demon may not only return but bring other demons back with it (see Matt. 12:43–45). Jesus says the final state of that person is then worse than before.

Because of this, ask God for discernment as to whether or not to address the demon(s) involved directly or to simply persist in intercessory prayer, seeking God's intervention in your child's heart and life. Ask God to make you aware of any attacks or assignments from hell against your child so you can pray against them quickly and effectively, and as often as necessary.

We would like to be more specific in describing

hands-on methods of fighting the enemy, but recognize that each person must be guided by the Holy Spirit. There are general battle tactics but God's Spirit must show you specifically how to enter combat. This will include the words you will use against demons to drive them out. You can't wage this kind of warfare with formulas. You must get direct guidance from the Lord. "In the same way, the Spirit helps us in our weakness. We do not know what we ought to pray for, but the Spirit himself intercedes for us with groans that words cannot express" (Rom. 8:26).

Fasting

If you run up against a particularly strong and stubborn spirit which refuses to leave your child—or your child does not wish it to leave—don't be discouraged. Remember, even the disciples in Jesus' day encountered this problem. Jesus explained their difficulty to cast out this particular demon this way: "This kind can come out by nothing but prayer and fasting" (Mark 9:29, NKJV). Powerful intercessory prayer often must precede any effective deliverance from demonic activity. Fasting enables this kind of prayer.

Some versions of the Bible do not include the words "and fasting" at the end of Mark 9:29 because some question exists as to whether those two words were included in the original manuscripts. However, Jesus did issue a mandate that His disciples would fast.

Jesus was once questioned as to why his disciples

did not fast. Jesus answered that his disciples had no need to fast while He was on earth with them, but that the time would come "when the bridegroom [Jesus] will be taken from them; then they *will* fast" (Matt. 9:14–15, italics added). Jesus is no longer physically present with us; therefore, it is the time that Jesus said his disciples "will fast." Notice He didn't say "should fast" or "can fast" or "may fast" or "might fast." His instructions were very explicit. If we call ourselves disciples, then fasting should be a regular part of our spiritual walk as surely as Bible reading and prayer.

Not a very popular subject, is it? No one likes to fast. Even those who have developed that discipline and can testify to the power and insight and growth gained during those times do not get excited about being hungry. "The spirit is willing, but the body is weak" (Mark 14:38) is never more true than when it comes to fasting. And yet fasting is one of the most powerful weapons available to us in spiritual warfare. In studying the lives of many of the great prayer warriors throughout history, we find that fasting was a part of their spiritual discipline.

One thing is for certain—you aren't the only one who hates the idea of fasting. Not only do most Christians recoil at the idea, the devil and his demons shudder in horror every time a saint passes up a meal in order to spend time in communion with God. They will pull out all the stops in an attempt to prevent you from completing your planned fast. They will:

- try to convince you that your headache is caused by hunger;
- tell you that you are really too weak and too frail to go without food;
- tell you your schedule is just too full and you need your strength to complete all that God has called you to do.

Remember James 4:7! "Submit yourselves, then, to God. Resist the devil, and he will flee from you." By determining to obey Jesus' mandate to fast, you are submitting yourself to God. Stand fast in that determination, and the devil will flee from you. The spiritual victories you will gain through fasting—both for yourself and those for whom you are praying—will far outweigh any temporary discomfort that may accompany your fast.

One warning is in order: The devil is so determined to keep you from fasting that, if he cannot stop you from beginning a fast, he will then tell you that you are not fasting long enough. He will tell you that if you were really spiritual, you would fast for two weeks, rather than two meals or two days. If you listen to him, you will only become discouraged when you cannot make it for two weeks and will then be tempted to discontinue fasting altogether.

Do not be deceived by his lies! Seek God for the amount of time He would have you fast. First Corinthians 10:13 assures us that God never requires of us more than we can bear. If you have peace that God is calling you to fast only one or two meals, then rest in that peace and do not let the enemy rob you of the benefits of that time spent with God.

The Battle Lines

Remember, there is a war going on, and the enemy has no scruples. He never calls or honors a truce, and there is no demilitarized zone. Everyone is either on God's side or on the devil's side. If you are on God's side—and you are if you have received Jesus as Savior—then you must "put on the full armor of God" (Eph. 6:11) and fight—for yourself, your children, your brothers and sisters in Christ, your friends, your neighbors, and for a world that is lost and dying in the grip of a cruel and vicious taskmaster.

Dr. James Dobson and Gary L. Bauer, authors of *Children at Risk,* declare that America is in the midst of a second civil war—and our children are the bounty over which the war is being waged. Newspaper columnist Patrick J. Buchanan agrees: "We Americans are locked in a cultural war for the soul of our country. . . . Are we any longer 'one nation, under God'; or has one-half of that nation already begun to secede from the other?"[1]

First Corinthians 16:13–14 warns us, "Be on your guard; stand firm in the faith; be men [and women] of courage; be strong. Do everything in love." What better principles to operate in when defending and rescuing our besieged children!

The time is growing short, and even as those of us

who "have longed for his [Jesus'] appearing" (2 Tim. 4:8) pray "Come, Lord Jesus" (Rev. 22:20), we must devote ourselves to the rescue of those still held captive by Satan's grasp—especially our children, those precious ones that God has given us as "a heritage from the LORD" (Ps. 127:3).

We cannot afford to lose that heritage by default—and we will not, so long as we lay hold of God's principles of doing everything in love (see 1 Cor. 16:14), even when that love requires painful sacrifice on our part. It is a sacrifice that will surely be rewarded with heartwarming returns.

Notes

Introduction

1. *Ventura Country Star-Free Press,* 10 June 1992, A-1.
2. Department of Justice, Federal Bureau of Investigation, *Uniform Crime Reports for the United States,* 1990.
3. U.S. Department of Health and Human Services, Public Health Service, Centers for Disease Control, *1991 Division of STD/HIV Prevention,* Annual Report, 13.
4. Department of Health and Human Services, National Center for Health Statistics.
5. Stanley K. Henshaw and Jennifer Van Vort, "Abortion Services in the United States, 1987 and 1988," *Family Planning Perspectives,* Vol. 22, No. 3, May/June 1990, 104.
6. National Center for Health Statistics.
7. *Los Angeles Times,* 4 November 1992, View section.
8. *Los Angeles Times,* 4 November 1992.

Chapter 1

1. *Los Angeles Times,* 4 November 1992, View section.
2. James Dobson, *Parenting Isn't for Cowards* (Dallas: Word, 1987), 13–14.

Chapter 5
1. Joe Klein, "Whose Values?" *Newsweek,* 8 June 1992.

Chapter 6
1. Paul Billheimer, *The Technique of Spiritual Warfare,* Trinity Broadcasting Network, 14.

Chapter 8
1. Dr. Kevin Leman & Randy Carlson, *Unlocking the Secrets of Your Childhood Memories* (Nashville: Thomas Nelson, 1989), 11.
2. Gary Smalley & John Trent, *The Blessing* (Nashville: Thomas Nelson, 1986).
3. Dr. James Dobson, *Hide or Seek* (Old Tappan: Revell, 1974), 15, 34.
4. Gordon Aeschliman, *Cages of Pain* (Dallas: Word, 1991), 25–26.

Chapter 9
1. If there is no support group available in your particular area, you can write to the following address for details on starting such a group: Kathi Mills, c/o South Coast Fellowship, 4050 Market St., Ventura, CA 93003.

Chapter 12
1. Information regarding this organization is available by writing: National Child Abuse Defense & Resource Center, P.O. Box 638, Holland, OH 43528, (419) 865–0513.

Chapter 13
1. *Los Angeles Times,* 11 September 1992.

About the Authors

Ray Beeson is founder and director of Overcomers Ministries, a teaching ministry emphasizing the subjects of spiritual warfare and prayer. A former high school and junior high school teacher, he has also been a youth pastor. In his early ministry he taught *Change the World School of Prayer* seminars under the direction of Dick Eastman. Ray lives in Ventura, California, with his wife Linda. They have four children.

An award-winning writer and former newspaper columnist, **Kathi Mills** has published ten books and numerous magazine articles. A frequent speaker at churches, women's groups and writer's conferences, Kathi is a licensed minister and serves on the pastoral care team at her church, South Coast Fellowship of Ventura, California, as a counselor and overseer of small-group ministries. Kathi also serves as chairman of the board of the Employment Aptitude and Placement Agency (EAPA) in Ventura, California. A mother and grandmother, Kathi lives in Santa Paula, California, with her husband Larry.